RETURN
of the
EAGLE

How America Saved Its National Symbol

Text by Greg Breining ■ *Photos by Frank Oberle and others*

The
Nature
Conservancy®
BOOKS FOR
CONSERVATION

FALCON™

Published in cooperation with The Nature Conservancy

Copyright © 1994 by Falcon Press Publishing Co., Inc.,
Helena and Billings, Montana

Editing, design, typesetting, and other prepress work
by Falcon Press, Helena, Montana.
Binding and printing in Korea.

Library of Congress Number 94-072402
ISBN 1-56044-300-6

For extra copies of this book please check with your local
bookstore, or write Falcon Press, P.O. Box 1718, Helena,
MT 59624. You may also call toll-free 1-800-582-2665.

FRANK OBERLE

CONTENTS

Incomparable for their grace, strength and beauty, eagles have been admired through the ages. Babylonians, Egyptians, Persians, Greeks, and Romans adopted the eagle as a symbol of earthly power and divine right. Native Americans revered our own native bald eagle for its power and keen eyesight. They coveted its feathers for headdresses and other ceremonial objects. And, of course, in 1782 the bald eagle was chosen as our national symbol.

The bald eagle's power and beauty impress us today, inspiring the legions of citizens who have helped to rescue this magnificent bird from the dark days of the 1960s, when the eagle's numbers in the lower forty-eight states had dwindled to fewer than 1,000 nesting birds and the bald eagle was declared an endangered species.

A mature bald eagle—America's greatest wildlife success story. FRANK OBERLE

A sentinel of the forest standing watch over the snowy landscape below. FRANK OBERLE

Pages 6-7: *First rays of sunlight shining through rising steam—a dramatic winter backdrop for a soaring bald eagle.*
LON E. LAUBER

Who are these benefactors of the bald eagle? They are the volunteers at the Gabbert Raptor Center at the University of Minnesota who swab out cages and tenderly care for injured birds. Their reward: a few moments of rapture as a rehabilitated eagle lifts from a gloved fist to fly free once again.

They include the Virginia officials who voted to ban a popular pesticide in 1991 because the chemical was killing the bald eagles that were repopulating that state.

They are enthusiastic birders throughout the country who count and record sightings of bald eagles to track how well the birds are faring.

They are citizens everywhere who viewed the disappearance of the bald eagle as a national tragedy, and who tirelessly worked, lobbied, and donated time and money to bring back America's living symbol of freedom.

Critical to the recovery of the bald eagle has been the work of The Nature Conservancy. In the late 1970s the Conservancy's Oregon field office acquired more than 1,000 acres in what would become the Bear Valley National Wildlife Refuge, which now hosts the largest wintering population of bald eagles in the lower forty-eight. A decade later, the Conservancy's Virginia chapter raised nearly $2 million to buy 3,500 acres of piney

Powerful wings quickly change direction in flight. FRANK OBERLE

woods along the James River to save the land from possible development. Today the James River Bald Eagle Refuge is the largest bald eagle roost east of the Mississippi. In virtually every state, the Conservancy has quietly and efficiently protected critical eagle habitat.

Through efforts such as these, the bald eagle's numbers have grown to some 8,000 nesting birds in the continental United States, and several tens of thousands of birds in Alaska and Canada.

This inspiring success story is told in *Return of the Eagle*. Author Greg Breining has drawn from the people most intimately involved with eagles to tell the story of their recovery. Photographer Frank Oberle has a deep personal connection to eagles. In addition to photographing the birds for nearly two decades, he and his wife, Judy, recently donated to The Nature Conservancy a 20-acre bald eagle roosting and feeding site on the Missouri shore of the Mississippi.

The uplifting message of *Return of the Eagle* is that we *can* rescue endangered species. May the bald eagle's strength, grace and tenacity inspire us to make the effort.

John C. Sawhill
President, The Nature Conservancy

Playing in the pastel skies of twilight after a summer storm. FRANK OBERLE

I N A LEAP OF FAITH, John Grobel launched his hang glider from a cliff overlooking the Mississippi near Red Wing, Minnesota. Jaws of bone-colored bluffs spread out below, as if to swallow him whole in the wide gulf of the river. As sun warmed the hills, thermals spiraled into the blue vault of the April sky.

Once aloft, Grobel noticed several large birds soaring in the distance. Turkey vultures, he thought. He enjoyed them. Never aggressive, they often let him fly in their midst. So Grobel tweaked his right rudder, banked his glider, and soared along the ridge, gaining altitude as he sailed toward the birds.

Soon he realized they weren't turkey vultures at all, but bald eagles—thirteen of them. As he approached, two adults—their white heads and tails now unmistakable—broke away from the group. Like interceptor aircraft, they sped toward the intruder. "I've got to get my camera," he thought. But he knew it was too late for that.

One eagle spun and flew twenty to thirty feet above Grobel's hang glider. The other wheeled and pulled in just a few feet from the right wing. Were the eagle a bit closer, Grobel could have reached

Wintering bald eagles perched in frost-covered trees—a common sight along the Chilkat River in Alaska. FRANK OBERLE

out and touched it. More than anything—more perhaps than the fan of the white tail, the seven-foot wingspan, or the powerful hooked beak—Grobel noticed the intense eye, a spot of yellow light as unflinching as the sun itself. Grobel felt the eye pierce him as if it were a needle.

Drawn to the birds, yet not wanting to frighten them, Grobel began simply to talk. He didn't know what else to do. As though they would understand, he explained he wanted to fly with them. He hoped the calm measure of his voice conveyed that he meant no harm.

Before long, the birds veered and headed back toward the group. "What have I got to lose?" Grobel thought, and he turned with them, hanging well back and slightly below the birds to avoid alarming them. The two sentinels led him back to the main flock. Amazingly, Grobel flew into their airspace. Suddenly he was surrounded by eagles, seven white-headed adults and six predominantly brown juveniles.

The birds were engaged in some sort of flight lesson. Several adults would single out a juvenile and escort it below the level of the bluffs, down toward the river, where the youngster apparently did not want to go. As it flapped and tried to climb back above the ridge, an adult would accompany it back downward, sometimes even

A mated pair taking advantage of a break in the weather. FRANK OBERLE

A fast and agile opportunist attempting to steal a fish from another eagle.
FRANK OBERLE

bumping it or pouncing on its back. Sometimes an adult would even fly under the young bird, spin upside down, lock talons with the other bird and pull it to a lower altitude. All the while, two adults shadowed Grobel's glider, watching his every move.

Finally, a half-hour after Grobel joined the flock, the eagles began to flap, quickly gaining altitude. They soared off down river toward Lake City, Minnesota. Grobel, quite unflappable, couldn't gain the altitude needed to follow. He watched them sail into the distance, with admiration and even envy for the efficiency and beauty of their flight. For several minutes, he simply glided back and forth along the ridge, marveling at what had happened and basking in the privilege he felt at having been able, however briefly, to fly with the most majestic birds he had ever seen.

Grobel isn't alone in his admiration of the eagle's grace and strength aloft—in Keats's words, its ability "to sleep wing-wide upon the air." Beauty in flight is characteristic of all the world's several dozen species of eagles, including our bald eagle, native to North America and the golden eagle, native to much of North America, Europe, and Asia. For what reason other than its majestic flight did the bald eagle serve as intermediary between the creator and the Ojibwa people? Why else did the Romans choose an eagle as the symbol to lead them to the far corners of their empire? And for what other reason did we choose the bald eagle as our national symbol? Because, simply, the eagle flies with the grace, power, and sheer majesty of few other birds, soaring high to the edge of sight, escaping our confined existence here on earth to become brother to the sun.

Unfortunately, the eagle's mastery aloft hasn't saved it from hard times here on earth. From an estimated tens of thousands of bald eagles in America in colonial days (and tens of thousands more in Canada and Alaska), the population in the lower forty-eight states dwindled to fewer than five hundred nesting pairs in 1963. Yet the magical spell that the eagle aloft casts on humans below proved its salvation, inspiring Americans to band together to save their national symbol from the serious threat of extinction. Through legislative action, research, government management, and the work of nonprofit groups and individual citizens, the bald eagle has been set on the road to recovery. In the process, Americans have demonstrated that endangered species can be saved—if people find the will to do so. And perhaps citizens have demonstrated something more—that in saving an endangered species, they can also find salvation from cynical neglect and narrow-minded pursuit of *more*.

A grizzly bear aggressively defending her cubs from the apparent attack of a bald eagle.
HENRY H. HOLDSWORTH

Eagles at the Chilkat Bald Eagle Preserve in Alaska—part of the single largest gathering of eagles in the world. ART WOLFE

A mature adult searching for rising trout.
JOHN HYDE

A two-year-old bald eagle attempting a precarious landing on a dead pine tree already occupied by a mature bird.
FRANK OBERLE

The last light of day—a beautiful backdrop for this eagle silhouette. FRANK OBERLE

Scanning open water for signs of food.
FRANK OBERLE

As Frank Oberle remarks, "This is America's greatest wildlife success story." Oberle, the chief photographer for this book and the driving force behind it, has spent countless hours in a blind along the icy shores of the Mississippi, drinking hot tea and warming numb fingers with his breath in order to photograph wintering eagles in intimate detail. In an act of sacrifice to the cause of the creature, Frank and his wife, Judy, donated twenty acres north of St. Louis to The Nature Conservancy as a bald eagle sanctuary and viewing area.

"We were a nation about to lose our symbol, and our symbol really reflects our soul," he observes. "If we don't value our symbol, our national emblem, then we are a nation doomed to fail. I think the reason everyone chipped in to save the eagle is that we were about to lose our soul. If we would have lost the eagle, we would have been a society of negligence and apathy and lack of pride. Even though other wildlife was in more danger, it was our soul at stake."

Such METAPHYSICS would have made perfect sense to earlier cultures around the world. The Bible speaks of the eagle's swiftness, grace, and strength of flight. Consort of Greek and Roman gods, only an eagle had the strength and speed to snatch Zeus's thunderbolts in its talons.

Eagles symbolized power in Babylon, Egypt, and Persia. The eagle was a sign of royalty throughout medieval Europe, from Munich to Constantinople. In Kirghizia, specially trained eagles—a subspecies of the golden eagle—were actually trained to hunt wolves.

The bald eagle, native only to North America, was sacred to many Native Americans. Eagles became totems, representing clans. Their feathers were used for ceremonial objects and headdresses. "Because of the eagle's importance to our people and because the eagle interceded for us at one time, it became the revered, sacred, and honored bird," says Larry Aitken, an Ojibwa historian and president of Leech Lake Tribal College in northern Minnesota. "It was the messenger of unconscious and conscious metaphysical ideas that pass between us. When eagles are soaring above or come to visit you, a lot of people believe they are reincarnations of people who come to watch over us and guide us."

For fifteen years Aitken worked with Jim Jackson, an Ojibwa medicine man. "He did spiritual ceremonies, pipe ceremonies, healing ceremonies," Aitken says. "He was a tremendously feeling and powerful man. I was fortunate to walk with him." Jackson would tell the following traditional legend about the bald eagle and the Ojibwa, known among themselves as Anishinabeg.

A mature bald eagle in the temperate rain forest of the Pacific Northwest. John Hyde

Long ago, Jackson would say, the earth operated in harmony. But then the Anishinabeg did some disrespectful things that angered the creator, who warned that all beings would be destroyed. Hearing this, the bald eagle was alarmed, because he was a friend of the Anishinabeg. The eagle volunteered to meet with the creator, even though the trip would require the eagle to fly very high where it might be burned by the sun.

Nonetheless, the eagle flew high toward the sun until it finally landed in the creator's world. "Who is walking in my world?" the creator asked. "It is Mi-Ge-Zi," the eagle answered. "Rather than destroy the Anishinabeg," the eagle suggested, "perhaps you could send teachers to instruct about their old ways of honor and respect."

The creator listened thoughtfully. "You speak bravely and with great wisdom," the creator said. "For your strong character and heroic act on behalf of Anishinabeg, from this day forth, everything that is yours will be honored and revered as sacred. Your image, your feathers, your claws will be as symbols and messages of connections and communications to my world. From now on, all those who respect and honor you will get special help from me."

"A lot of times when I'm going to go somewhere, I'll get out early in the morning and look and a big bald eagle will fly right over me," says Aitken. "I'll tell my wife, 'Polly, I think Jimmy came by to bid me good travel and watch me.' "

MORE RECENT ARRIVALS to America's shores could also admire the creature. Congress voted the bald eagle the national emblem of the new nation in 1782, five years before the Constitution would be drafted. Thomas Jefferson lauded the eagle as "a free spirit, high soaring and courageous." American ornithologist Alexander Wilson wrote:

High o'er the watery uproar, silent seen,
Sailing sedate in majesty serene,
Now midst the pillared spray sublimely lost,
And now, emerging, down the rapids tossed,
Glides the Bald Eagle, gazing, calm and slow.

Yet a contravening and heavily anthropomorphic attitude was also lodged in Western thought. The Dutch Renaissance scholar Erasmus called the eagle "a bird neither beautiful nor musical nor good for food, but murderous, greedy, hateful to all, the curse of all, and with its great powers of doing harm only surpassed by its desire to do it."

Erasmus spoke, of course, about a European species of raptor, not our own noble bald eagle. Yet founding father Benjamin Franklin wrote no more charitably about our native bird: "I wish the bald eagle had not been chosen as the representative of our country. He is a bird of bad moral character; like those among men who live by sharping and robbing, he is generally poor, and often very lousy."

Even when John James Audubon set out to learn about America's birds, science still knew little of the eagle. In fact, on a trip up the Mississippi in 1814, Audubon apparently misidentified a juvenile bald eagle, not realizing that immature birds, though fully grown, don't acquire the distinctive white head and tail until their fourth or fifth year. Proclaiming the bird "a species quite new to me," he dubbed it the Washington sea eagle. A spectacular bird it was, according to Audubon, with a wingspan exceeding ten feet. "The mightiest of the feathered tribe," it was every bit as heroic as its namesake, the country's first president. "If America has reason to be proud of her Washington, so has she to be proud of her great Eagle," wrote Audubon.

Enamored as he was of his fictional bird, Audubon couldn't hide his disdain for the bald eagle: "They exhibit a great degree of cowardice. Suffer me, kind reader, to say how much I grieve that it should have been selected as the Emblem of my Country."

A dramatic panorama in the setting sun.
FRANK OBERLE

26

hundreds of feet above the water, or spy a rabbit a
mile away, and then dive, if necessary, up to one
hundred miles an hour. Even from an easy dive,
an eagle strikes prey with a powerful blow. Strong,
sharp talons, with nearly the span of the human
hand, clutch and carry prey with power. The
massive beak tears apart flesh and bones.

The bald eagle's mainstay is fish, dead or alive.
Eagles perch above a shoreline, swooping low over
the water to snatch a fish floating, floundering, or
swimming near the surface. On windy days, eagles
may soar above a lee shore, monitoring the surface for fish the waves wash toward land.

The hunter. FRANK OBERLE

A graceful landing atop a pine tree. FRANK OBERLE

Yet the bird's tastes are eclectic. Eagles often scavenge on road-killed deer. On the West Coast they pick away at beached whales. Researchers in Minnesota reported that while most nests they visited were littered with the remains of fish, one contained almost entirely turtle shells. John Mathisen, wildlife biologist for the Chippewa National Forest in northern Minnesota, reports finding a flea market of items in bald eagle nests. Most common are fish. (Sometimes eaglets are pierced by hooks or lures, or are tangled in monofilament fishing line.) Also common are ducks. Mathisen has found the remains of a great blue heron, a bird nearly as large as an adult eagle. But what most surprised Mathisen were a pair of coveralls and men's briefs.

In their world of predation, bald eagles often steal from one another, especially in the winter when they gather around open water and a source of fish. The larger, more dominant—and often the hungrier—birds often will stalk over to an eagle eating nearby and commandeer the meal.

Eagles also steal meals from gulls and ospreys. Typically, an eagle will harass an osprey until the smaller bird drops its catch, which the eagle may intercept in midair or pick up off the ground or water. In *The Bald Eagle: Haunts and Habits of a Wilderness Monarch*, Canadian biologist Gary R.

Diving at incredible speed toward its prey.
JOHN HYDE

Bortolotti writes of the following eagle-osprey encounter: "On each pass the osprey visibly flinched, for the eagle's talons barely cleared its back. After three unsuccessful attacks, the eagle turned to brute force. This time coming up fast from behind and below, the eagle flipped onto its back, thrust its talons upward, and ripped the fish right out of the osprey's grasp."

Sometimes the bird itself is the target. One day Michael C. Tritel stepped out of the Carnelian Bay Laundromat on California Route 28. Waiting for his laundry to dry, he scanned the shore of Lake Tahoe, just across the highway, and spotted a bald eagle with his binoculars. Eagles appeared on the lake nearly every winter. As he crossed the road, he began to see rafts of mallards, a few Canada geese foraging on shore, and far out on the lake, several gulls bobbing on the waves. Suddenly the birds near land took wing. Within seconds, Tritel saw the eagle soaring along the shoreline. He locked his binoculars on the bird. For several minutes he admired the eagle as it glided in tight circles, falling toward the lake and rising once again on the gusty wind. Without warning, the gulls scattered, taking flight in all directions. Through his binoculars, Tritel watched a single gull hang in view. The eagle apparently spotted it too, gliding low to the water toward the other bird. The two

A large female showing her weight of fourteen pounds and wing span of seven feet. FRANK OBERLE

Playing in the warm thermals of a summer afternoon. FRANK OBERLE

birds began to circle one another. What a stupid gull, thought Tritel, thinking the gull was trying to pester the eagle. But as the avian minuet continued, Tritel realized the eagle was the pursuer. The eagle swooped upward, half folded its wings and suddenly dove, flexing its talons and knocking the gull to the water. As the eagle circled overhead, the dazed gull recovered and took off from the lake. Once again the eagle dropped from the sky and knocked the gull to the water. Then, instead of plucking the gull from the water, as Tritel expected, the eagle perched on the stunned gull while holding its own wings above the waves. For fifteen seconds or more, the eagle held the gull underwater. Then, finally, the eagle labored upward, carrying the drowned gull in its talons.

Eagles on Alaska's Petrel Island have been known to dig sea birds such as puffins, auklets, and storm petrels from their burrows, ambushing the nocturnal birds at burrow entrances, and chasing them down on foot at night. One observer told of watching an eagle repeatedly swoop after a swimming coot, which dove each time the eagle passed overhead. Finally, the eagle became so provoked it dove underwater after the coot and stayed submerged several seconds—so long, it seemed to have drowned. Finally it burst to the surface with the coot in its talons. Then, water-

soaked and burdened with its prey, the eagle lumbered from the water, its wings touching the surface for several dozens of yards before it gained altitude, and landed on the lowest limb of a tree along shore. Sometimes eagles become so waterlogged they must use their wings to swim to shore.

Like wolves on the wing, eagles occasionally team up. In a valley near Provo, Utah, researcher Clyde Edwards watched wintering bald eagles take turns swooping low over brush to flush rabbits from their cover. Eagles even stalked through the scrub on foot to dislodge rabbits from their hiding spots.

One October day, Jane Whitledge and her husband, Doran, were drinking tea at their campsite in northern Minnesota's Boundary Waters Canoe Area Wilderness when a lone snow goose whistled overhead. On its tail were two bald eagles, stroking the air with strong, measured wing beats. Off they disappeared, over the ridge behind camp. Soon a third eagle flew into sight, glided over the ridge, and suddenly dove after the other birds. Curious to see what had become of the goose, Jane and Doran crashed through the underbrush and, perhaps fifteen minutes after seeing the goose, finally topped the ridge. Nothing. As they walked along the hill, an eagle flapped slowly from a pine. Below the branch where the eagle sat, the

Aerial acrobatics, usually interpreted as courtship, but may instead serve to define territory. FRANK OBERLE

36

Whitledges found the head and wings of the goose, lying on a pillow of its own feathers.

"They hunt just like a squadron," says photographer Frank Oberle, who remembers watching eagles and snow geese from an airplane over Mark Twain National Wildlife Refuge at the confluence of the Mississippi and Illinois rivers. A raft of geese had lifted off the water, leaving behind an apparently injured bird. Soon an eagle soared into view. As the eagle swooped down on the cripple, the goose dove out of reach. The goose popped to the surface for air and dove again as the eagle made another pass. So it went, the goose always eluding the eagle and catching its breath before the eagle could circle and try again. Soon, however, another eagle joined the attack. Then two more. Before long, seven or eight eagles circled above the goose. Oberle and his pilot flew at a distance, fascinated. "When one forced it down, by the time it got up another one was right there in the pattern to strafe it," Oberle recalls. "Each time we went around in a circle, we could see a few feathers coming out of that goose. By the time we left there was a pile of feathers on the water." Fearing they were disturbing the natural event unfolding below them, Oberle and his pilot decided to move off. But, says Oberle, "I know they killed that goose."

Sharing wintering habitat with bald eagles along the Mississippi River, Oberle has often watched eagles dive for fish and make a meal of unwary gulls. He has watched eagles stoop on other eagles and strike one another with open talons in squabbles over food and feeding locations. Yet the most impressive displays of an eagle's aerial prowess have come on those transitory days that dare whisper the end of winter, with the ice just out of the river and the wind out of the south. Then eagles begin soaring above the bluffs. One executes a barrel roll and soars back up to the heights. Soon two begin to circle. One dives beneath the other, rolls onto its back and clutches talons with the other bird. The eagles cartwheel over and over and over, tumbling down toward the river until Oberle expects them crash into the bluff. "The clinching interlocking claws, a living, fierce, gyrating wheel," wrote Walt Whitman in "The Dalliance of Eagles"—

Four beating wings, two beaks,
a swirling mass tight grappling,
In tumbling turning clustering loops,
straight downward falling,
Till o'er the river pois'd, the twain yet one,
a moment's lull,
A motionless still balance in the air,
then parting, talons loosing,
Upward again on slow-firm pinions slanting,
their separate diverse flight,
She hers, he his, pursuing.

A wintering bald eagle in Tule Lake
National Wildlife Refuge, California.
HENRY H. HOLDSWORTH

Eagles' aerobatics are usually interpreted as courtship, though they may also serve to define territory. We don't know. And for whatever reason, eagles will fly back and forth high above the river, playing keep away with a stick the size of a baton. Occasionally one grabs it out of another's talons or drops it from on high and then stoops at great speed, plummeting down, gaining on the stick, and catching it in midair. "They'll do these wonderful little things," Oberle remarks. "It only lasts for a week, a week and a half. Then they're gone. I'm sure they do that all the way back up the river."

Whittle HEN EUROPEAN SETTLERS FIRST sailed to America's shores, eagles soared, nested, and fished along the Atlantic from Labrador to the tip of south Florida, and along the Pacific from Baja California to Alaska. Eagles inhabited every large river and concentration of lakes in the interior of the continent. They nested in forty-five of the lower forty-eight states. As recently as the late nineteenth century, one researcher estimated an eagle nest for every mile of shore along Chesapeake Bay. Wintering birds congregated on the lower Hudson. Eagles were extremely abundant along coastal Maine. According to researchers Jon M. Gerrard and Gary R. Bortolotti, bald eagles may have

Eagles silhouetted against Alaska's setting sun. FRANK OBERLE

numbered a half million before the arrival of the European settlers.

In fact, eagles were so common they were regarded as pests or vermin. In Cumberland County, Maine, according to a 1668 account, an "infinite number" were shot to feed hogs. In the nineteenth century, eagles were shot on Long Island. Alaska offered a bounty on the birds from 1917 to 1952; more than one hundred thousand were shot.

And Audubon himself, patron saint of bird watchers and namesake of one of the country's foremost environmental groups, hunted eagles for specimens, sport, and, apparently, food. He reported in a letter from a trip up Florida's St. Johns River in 1832 that he had "two frolics at Shooting White headed Eagles and killed 5 in 24 hours which is more than most Sportsmen can boast of." Audubon wrote 7 February 1832, "They proved good eating, the flesh resembling veal in taste and tenderness."

Later settlers shot eagles with a vengeance. Barton Evermann of Illinois said in 1888, "Scarcely does an eagle come into our State now and get away alive." Out west, traps and poisoned bait set for wolves and coyotes often killed eagles instead. Not that most ranchers cared, and after the wolf was extirpated, they turned their attention to eagles directly. Western ranchers mounted a campaign against both bald and, to a greater extent, golden eagles, killing an estimated twenty thousand between 1950 and 1970. In the early twentieth century, Indians hunted eagles—prized for their feathers—to near extinction in the Wichita Mountains in southern Oklahoma, according to J.H. Gaut. In Florida, wrote Oscar Baynard in 1913, "every hog raiser in the county kills every one he can on account of the Eagle's perverted taste for razor back pig." (Though Baynard didn't explain what is so perverted about a taste for ham, he echoed the belief that eagles had a thing for pigs. John Lawson reported in 1709 that one pig carried off by an eagle stirred up "such a noise overhead that strangers had thought there were flying sows and pigs.")

Not only did we shoot eagles; we tried to starve them. The destruction of eastern and Great Lakes riverine fisheries through dam-building, logging, and pollution decimated the eagle's food supply. The loss of bison on the American prairies eliminated a major source of carrion. The extinction of passenger pigeons and the loss of the continent's tremendous waterfowl flocks also reduced the food available to eagles. The logging of Great Lakes pineries destroyed the towering white pines where eagles so often built their nests.

Because of the slaughter and loss of food and

Spotting a fish from hundreds of feet above the water or spying a rabbit a mile away with eyesight six to eight times sharper than ours. FRANK OBERLE

44

Making a pass over water in search of herring. JOHN HYDE

A mature eagle perched in old-growth forest. ART WOLFE

Pages 46-47: *An immature bald eagle flying over the Bering Sea and Aleutian Islands off the coast of Alaska.* LON E. LAUBER

A roost amid spring flowers. Lynn M. Stone

Soaring—with mastery and control. Lon E. Lauber

Attempting a rollover before diving in an aerial courtship display. FRANK OBERLE

habitat, eagles began to disappear during the nineteenth and twentieth centuries. Even in Canada's rugged interior, the eagle was "nothing more than a rare, interesting, and picturesque feature of the landscape," wrote P.A. Taverner in *Birds of Canada* in 1953.

In 1940 the federal Bald Eagle Protection Act helped to protect the bald eagle from direct persecution (except in Alaska, where the bounty remained for twelve more years). Construction of locks and dams on the Mississippi and Missouri rivers during the 1920s and '30s created new winter feeding areas by keeping sections of the rivers below the dams from freezing over. Evidence suggested the bald eagle population of the continental United States was beginning to rebound. But a strange, new danger, discovered shortly after World War II, threatened not simply to once again reduce the numbers of the bald eagle, but to drive it to extinction.

The danger: DDT and similar pesticides. Their deadly effect on bald eagles was documented by Charles Broley, a retired bank manager from Winnipeg, Manitoba. In 1939, Broley enthusiastically undertook a project for the National Audubon Society to band eaglets in Florida nests to study their migration as adults. By the early 1940s, he had found 125 active eagle nests

An easy dive. FRANK OBERLE

along Florida's Gulf Coast. Despite hardships—one rambunctious eagle sunk the talons of one foot into Broley's hand while spanning his face from crown to chin with the other—Broley was banding 150 eagles a season.

But in 1947 he noticed fewer eaglets. That year, 41 percent of occupied nests failed to produce any young at all. The number of failures grew each year, reaching 78 percent in 1950. Year after year, the number of successful nests declined. Looking back through his notes, Broley found that in 1946, along a 100-mile stretch of coast from Tampa to Englewood, he recorded fifty-six nests with 103 young. In 1957 he found only seven nests with eight young. In 1958 Broley drove 100 miles down the coast before finding the single eaglet he banded.

"I am firmly convinced," he reported in *Audubon Magazine*, "that about 80 percent of the Florida bald eagles are sterile." Broley realized that Florida eagles eat primarily fish and that scientists recently had learned that pesticides such as DDT, sprayed enthusiastically after the war, could cause sterility in some animals. Evidence also was mounting that DDT and other pesticides polluted water supplies and eventually entered the food chain, passing from one animal to another. "An eagle is naturally going to catch the most sluggish fish and is it not possible that a cumulative amount of DDT in eagles has caused sterility?" Broley asked. Florida wasn't alone. Eagle watchers in the Midwest reported few young eagles. And when Broley tried to band eagles near his Ontario cottage, he discovered widespread nesting failure. "Our American bald eagle—national emblem of this country—is a very sick bird," he concluded.

Broley died in 1959, just a year after his landmark report in *Audubon*. But "there was quite a lot of interest in Broley's information," recalls Alexander "Sandy" Sprunt IV, then Audubon's director of research. "The fact of the rapid drop in eagle production got people pretty excited about the whole thing. The Fish and Wildlife Service didn't have any money at that time—this was before the Endangered Species Act—but there was so much interest in what was happening to the bald eagle, that the National Audubon Society said, well, we would take a crack at it."

So in 1960 the conservation group launched its Continental Bald Eagle Project, working closely with the Fish and Wildlife Service. "We set out to find out what was happening to bald eagles," Sprunt says. "When we started, no one knew for sure that DDT was the problem. We set out to find how many eagles there were, where they were, how they were reproducing."

Slowing forward momentum to catch a fish on the surface of a river. FRANK OBERLE

53

Wings meant to glide. Frank Oberle

Sprunt surveyed eagle watchers throughout the country. State and federal game management agencies provided particularly good information about bald eagle numbers and nesting sites. Sprunt also flew over the Mississippi and Missouri rivers to search for wintering eagles and took failed eggs from nests for examination and chemical analysis.

Sprunt's work reinforced Broley's suspicions. "We found out for sure that the different populations of eagles were breeding at different rates," Sprunt says. "If you averaged out the production of a population of eagles and the amount of DDT in the eggs, it was a direct correlation."

Second, the Continental Bald Eagle Project confirmed that eagle numbers were alarmingly low, especially in the eastern United States. In Maine, once an eagle haven, "the situation was very bad. Chesapeake was not too good. The Lake States varied a lot. The birds on the shores of Lake Superior, for instance, were practically producing nothing, whereas the ones farther inland were doing better."

In 1963 Sprunt tabulated fewer than five hundred nesting pairs of bald eagles in the entire lower forty-eight states. The count "undoubtedly was low" but nonetheless suggested the eagle's plight was critical.

The good news, if any was to be found, was this: First, in Alaska and the Pacific Northwest, "eagles were coming out of your ears, like English sparrows,"

The bald eagle, one of eleven species of fish and sea eagles in the world, native only to North America. FRANK OBERLE

Using its tail as rudder to ready for a swift descent. FRANK OBERLE

58

Watching over a pair of week-old eaglets.
LON E. LAUBER

An immature bald eagle in the rain forests of the Northwest. JOHN HYDE

Sprunt says. Second, unlike the peregrine falcon, the bald eagle had not completely disappeared from historical strongholds. However sick populations were, they continued to struggle on.

As the U.S. Fish and Wildlife Service demonstrated through its work at Patuxent Wildlife Research Center in Maryland, DDT and related compounds accumulated in bald eagles. The chemicals interfered with calcium metabolism, causing the birds to lay eggs with paper-thin shells. Parent birds crushed their future young as they nested.

In 1967 the bald eagle was classified as a federal endangered species throughout the lower forty-eight states, except in Minnesota, Wisconsin, Michigan, Oregon, and Washington, where it was listed as threatened, a less critical designation. Because of the designation, federal and state governments took renewed interest in protecting eagle habitat.

Endangered species designation was vitally important to the eagle. But perhaps the most seminal event in eagle conservation had occurred five years earlier. In 1962 Rachel Carson's *Silent Spring* appeared, warning readers in this country and around the world that a "chemical barrage has been hurled against the fabric of life.... Science has armed itself with the most modern and terrible weapons, and that in turning them against the in-sects it has also turned them against the earth." Beautiful, methodical, solid, and alarming, *Silent Spring* motivated citizens like few other works of environmental literature. Partly in response to the uproar caused by Carson's book, DDT was banned by Canada in 1970 and by the United States two years later.

THE EFFECT OF BANNING DDT was profound and nearly immediate. In eagle strongholds, eagles began to increase dramatically. In the greater Yellowstone ecosystem, for example, the number of breeding pairs rose from about thirty when the ban took hold to more than fifty just ten years later. In northern Minnesota's Chippewa National Forest, nesting success climbed from less than fifty percent in the 1960s to eighty percent by the 1980s.

Yet in many areas, DDT had already caused bald eagles to vanish. Because eagles tend to nest where they first learned to fly and hunt, they are slow to colonize new areas. So, many wildlife managers chose to recolonize former eagle range through reintroductions.

In New York, for example, eagles were killed in the 1800s to protect dwindling stocks of brook and lake trout. White pine forests were logged, depriving eagles of nesting trees. Bald eagles were

Poised for the first flight of the day. FRANK OBERLE

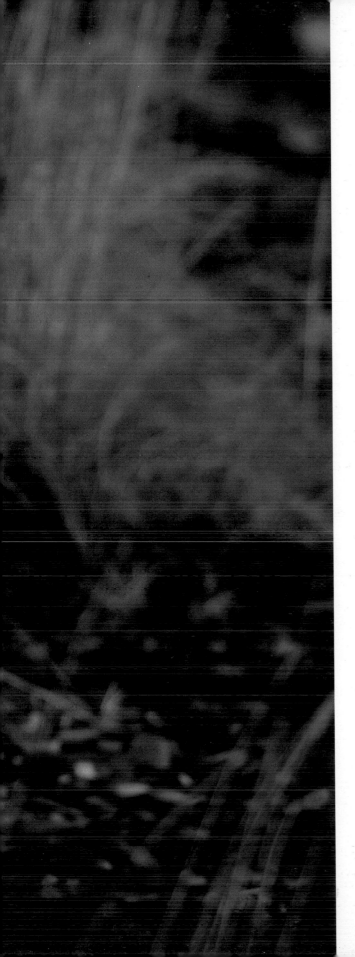

probably rare by 1850. By 1976, according to Peter Nye, one pair nested—unsuccessfully—in the entire state.

Rather than wait for eagles to recolonize on their own, Nye, who now heads the Endangered Species Unit of the New York State Division of Fish and Wildlife, decided to hurry nature along. He became a pioneer in the reintroduction technique known as "hacking." Nye and his assistants raised young birds obtained from Alaska and the Great Lakes states, where eagles were still plentiful. Soon they moved the chicks to nesting platforms, or "hacking towers," in the woods. The researchers continued to feed the chicks, which were still confined to the towers. Once the eaglets were old enough to fly, the bars came down. They would learn to fly and forage through instinct. That was the theory.

Nye hacked two eagles in central New York in 1976. Seven years later the two birds nested successfully less than one hundred miles from where they were released. In 1983 Nye hacked twenty-three eaglets in the Adirondacks. Since then, Nye's program has released 198 eagles. They form the nucleus of New York's population, presently about two dozen nesting pairs. Hacking has helped states such as Indiana to restore bald eagles to areas where they had virtually disappeared.

The George Miksch Sutton Avian Research

Watching for prey from a good vantage point. FRANK OBERLE

63

Center of Bartlesville, Oklahoma, tried a different approach to hacking. Workers there obtained their eaglets by taking eggs—all the eggs—from nests. "In most birds of prey, if you take the eggs of the entire clutch, they'll lay a second clutch," explains Alan Jenkins, the center's assistant director. "If we took a hundred eggs, that would have hardly any impact at all, as opposed to a hundred chicks." A hundred chicks would have devastated the South's precarious eagle population.

But eagle eggs were hard to come by. No eagles at all nested in Oklahoma. So in 1983 Sutton director Steve Sherrod asked Florida wildlife officials for permission to sneak eggs from nests in northern and central Florida, the only southern state where eagles were plentiful enough to risk this novel experiment. Many biologists doubted the eagles would "recycle," or lay a second clutch. And many doubted the Sutton center would be able to successfully hatch and raise eaglets for eventual release.

The task of strapping on climbing spurs and scampering up tall southern pines fell to Wayne Norton, a Gainesville, Florida, tree surgeon. "It's more than exhilaration, sir, it's fear! Often these nests are precariously put into the very top branches, the outermost branches of the tree." The nest, a thatch of sticks that may easily exceed a

ton, looks as though a beaver decided to build its lodge in a tree. "There are very few substantial limbs that will support a climber's weight. You test. Then you test with a little weight. Then you add a little more weight. Then you just hold your breath and get on up there." He would wear a mask and gloves to protect the eggs from contamination as he loaded them into a foam-lined plastic pipe. Usually he scored two or three. Rarely he recovered four, and just once he found five. "You don't really have to worry about the eagles," he says. The parents may dive at a climber but rarely make contact. The wind is something else. Once on Lake George, a gust blew Norton from a nest. He dropped the length of his safety rope and dangled far above the ground.

Once lowered to the ground, the eggs are slipped into a portable incubator. After eaglets hatch, they are fed with an eagle hand puppet to ensure they imprint on their own kind, not on human handlers. After two months, the young are mustered out to hacking towers. After two weeks, the birds are allowed to try their developing wings and, finally, to fly free.

According to Jenkins, about eighty percent of the "donor" eagles laid second clutches. And a University of Florida study showed that Sutton's carefully conducted egg harvest has had no effect on Florida's eagle population. Meanwhile, Sutton

Grabbing a fish from the water on an early morning fishing attempt. FRANK OBERLE

65

Poised to strike a fish in the water. JOHN HYDE

The distinctive white head and tail showing the eagle's sexual maturity—usually reached by its fourth or fifth year. Frank Oberle

Soaring above Alaska's Chilkat Bald Eagle Preserve. Frank Oberle

ingested fishing lures from dead or dying fish they pick up."

"We have seen a lot of lead poisoning," Redig says. Eagles most often pick up lead by eating waterfowl wounded by hunters. Redig often sees the symptoms of acute lead poisoning: weakness, lethargy, weight loss, green diarrhea. Lead pellets show up clearly in X-rays. This evidence was used by the National Wildlife Federation, which sued the U.S. Fish and Wildlife Service in 1985 to force the agency to phase out the use of lead shot in many waterfowling areas. Now duck hunters must load their guns with nontoxic steel. Waterfowl continue to pick up lead pellets that have sat for years in the mucky bottoms of duck marshes. So the problem of lead poisoning hasn't disappeared.

"Lead is toxic at any level in the body," Redig says. "It does beg the question, is there some relationship between low-level lead poisoning and other injury problems we see in bald eagles? They may perhaps have problems with efficiency in normal foraging so they scavenge on road kills and get clobbered by cars."

Another threat to eagles is the "unholy mix" of pesticides, heavy metals, PCBs, and various organic poisons virtually ubiquitous in the environment, Redig says. One of the most deadly, and problematic for eagles, has been carbofuran, a poison farmers throughout the country spread on corn, rice, and other crops to kill root-killing nematodes and insects. Virginia banned the poison in 1991, after it was discovered to have killed several thousand birds, including a bald eagle and its eaglet. Elsewhere, the chemical is highly restricted. But that didn't save at least seventeen bald eagles poisoned by carbofuran in northwestern Wisconsin in early 1994. A federal official told *U.S. News and World Report* recently that western ranchers use a variety of poisons to kill as many as two thousand to three thousand bald and golden eagles each year.

Other poisons are more insidious. Research on Wisconsin's Lake Superior shoreline indicates eagles nesting near the lake have up to ten times greater concentrations of PCBs and DDE (a byproduct of DDT) in their blood than eagles just a few miles inland. There's evidence too that shoreline birds have a much tougher time reproducing. Other research suggests that many pesticides and complex industrial pollutants mimic the effects of estrogens and other natural hormones that control bodily development. Their presence may cause birth defects, infertility, and other abnormalities—not only in bald eagles and other wildlife, but also, perhaps, in humans.

Serious though these problems are, they've not prevented a bald eagle recovery, Redig observes.

Parachuting to grab a fish from the water.
Frank Oberle

Gliding effortlessly through the sky.
Frank Oberle

"The bald eagle population, despite all that, with the management protection given to it under the Endangered Species Act, has done incredibly well."

Periodically, the Raptor Center releases its recovered raptors. Besides making terrific photo opportunities, the sight of an eagle flying free once more provides infinite rewards to the 150 volunteers who donate twenty thousand hours to the center each year, swabbing out bird quarters and leading tours. "This is an avenue of involvement for them with conservation," Redig says. "They become real advocates for what we're doing. I make no arguments at all that the rehabilitation work we've done has had any direct impact on the bald eagle population. But it has had a tremendous impact on people's attitudes, understanding, and appreciation for bald eagles and the very nature of the problems we do unwittingly create."

W HEN CHARLES BROLEY first banded eagles in Florida, he noted the explosion of housing developments in prime eagle nesting areas. He dismissed the loss of habitat as "a minor factor" in comparison to DDT poisoning. But as the threat of DDT has diminished and humans' appetite for land increases, the ravening plunder of the eagles' habitat has become the most serious threat.

Since Broley's pioneering work, eagle nesting and nesting habitat have most concerned conservationists. Important early work occurred in the Chippewa National Forest, along the headwaters of the Mississippi, where the river is a rippling forest stream with little evidence of its impending grandeur. This tall-pine and lake country has one of the highest densities of breeding eagles in the United States. Even during the dark days of the 1950s and '60s, the 1.6-million-acre Chippewa harbored more than twenty pairs of breeding birds.

Eagles shared the Chippewa with loggers, fishermen, cabin owners, and tourists. John Mathisen, the forest's young biologist, knew it was vital to protect this eagle nesting stronghold from disturbance. He realized that loss of nesting trees could seriously affect the eagle population. The construction of logging roads and even disturbance by hikers and campers could drive eagles away from a nest.

So in the early 1960s, Mathisen began to track the number and nesting success of bald eagles in the forest. He also began to develop a method of protecting individual bald eagle nests that serves as a model for many land management agencies today.

Mathisen recorded the precise location of each nest. Most sat in the so-called supercanopy white pine and red pine—the aged giants that tower above the other trees of the forest. Often the uppermost branches were dead and bare, providing a platform for the huge nest and landing space for an incoming bird with a seven-foot wingspan. Usually the eagles chose a tree near a lake or open meadow. For each nest, Mathisen noted the type and size of tree that supported it, described the surrounding habitat, and identified nearby activities, such as logging or recreation, that might disturb nesting eagles. He'd even take low-level aerial photos to establish a record of the forest cover and land use. Finally, he'd establish a buffer zone around each nest, permitting no activity at all within one hundred meters, and some restrictions, especially during nesting, up to a half-mile away. Though laborious and time-consuming, the protection has paid off, says Mathisen. Once DDT was banned, the number of nesting eagles increased nearly tenfold, to almost two hundred pairs by 1993.

Federal and state agencies have acted to protect nesting eagles on public land. Yet many prime nesting spots occupy private ground, where they may be lost to logging or development. Often, government hasn't been able to act quickly enough to spare the land. Sometimes, agencies are simply too broke to buy. Fortunately, private conservation

Five adult birds taking advantage of a raised perch. LYNN M. STONE

76

groups such as The Nature Conservancy have often stepped forward to buy land to protect it.

Along Maine's craggy seacoast, where flocks of bald eagles once soared, pesticides nearly destroyed the population. In 1965 four eaglets fledged in Maine. Recovery has been slow. Barely more than one hundred eagles survive today. The Nature Conservancy has been working with the Maine Coast Heritage Trust, local towns, private landowners, and the Maine Bureau of Public Lands and Department of Inland Fisheries and Wildlife to protect the forty-five islands of the Great Wass Island Archipelago. The Conservancy itself has purchased and protected more than a dozen islands with bald eagle nesting and summer roosting sites.

The Conservancy's Louisiana Field Office recently purchased 547 acres just outside New Orleans to establish its White Kitchen Preserve, a sprawling complex of freshwater marsh and cypress-tupelo swamp named for the restaurant that once overlooked the property from U.S. 90. High up in one tree is a stick nest the size of a Volkswagen, tended for seventy years by successive generations of bald eagles.

The Conservancy's Virginia Chapter raised nearly $2 million to buy 3,500 acres along the James River near Hopewell. The land has been sold to the U.S. Fish and Wildlife Service and, with recent additions of land, now forms the James River National Wildlife Refuge. Surrounded by burgeoning development spreading out from Richmond, the refuge harbors three active bald eagle nests and more than 125 roosting and feeding eagles during the summer, making it one of the largest summer roosts in the eastern United States.

In Michigan's Upper Peninsula, Ford Motor Company will continue to lease sixty-seven acres to the Conservancy for as long as eagles nest on the site. The Conservancy's Michigan chapter also protects 2,168 acres of bald eagle habitat in its Erie Marsh Preserve. But emblematic of the Great Lakes' continuing pollution problems, the first eaglet produced on the site in years was born with a crossed-over bill. The deformity, probably caused by contaminants in fish, would have doomed the eaglet to starve had it been left in the wild.

The Conservancy protects bald eagle habitat in other states as well. The organization purchased 1,889-acre Otter Island for the South Carolina Wildlife and Marine Resources Department. The Oklahoma Chapter has teamed up with local Audubon chapters and state and federal agencies to establish the Arkansas River Bald Eagle Preserve. Landowners sign a nonbinding registry agreement indicating they won't alter eagle habitat. A recent registry now

79

Part of the November-December congregation of 5,000 bald eagles along the Chilkat River, Alaska. LYNN M. STONE

supports a nest built by two eagles raised and released several years ago by the George Miksch Sutton Avian Research Center.

Florida, location of some of the country's most intense development pressure, is home also to some of its most extensive eagle nesting preserves. Working with local watershed management districts, the state, and the U.S. Fish and Wildlife Service, the Conservancy has helped protect hundreds of thousands of acres of lake and river shoreline, marshes, and swamps that provide habitat for bald eagles, Florida panthers, and other endangered creatures.

The organization worked with the Walt Disney World Co. to protect 8,500 acres of pine flatwoods, oak scrub, and mesic hammocks lying between Lake Russell and Lake Hatchineha south of Orlando. With new additions of land, the site, now called Disney Wilderness Preserve, will total more than eleven thousand acres. Six pairs of bald eagles nest on the property. The site also provides habitat for the federally endangered wood stork, and the federally threatened Florida scrub jay, crested caracara, eastern indigo snake, and American alligator.

The preserve got its start when Disney asked state, federal, and local authorities permission to develop 500 acres of wetlands at Walt Disney

A 23-day-old eaglet waiting for a parent to bring its next meal to the nest. Eugene F. O'Neill

A fledgling bald eagle and its mother in a nest at Cross Lake, Minnesota. Lon E. Lauber

81

World. Agencies approved—if Disney agreed to purchase what was then known as Walker Ranch, a working cattle ranch and hunting camp being held for commercial development. Disney bought the land in 1992 and is turning ownership over to the Conservancy in stages. The conservation group plans to build an environmental learning center on the site.

The Disney preserve is flanked by residential and commercial development. From his office window, preserve director Steve Gatewood watches homes go up. The surrounding population will complicate the Conservancy's efforts to manage meadows and scrub lands with controlled burning. On the bright side, says Gatewood, "We're going to have a neighborhood constituency. We're going to recruit some of those people to volunteer here and become the advocates to protect the preserve."

No LESS IMPORTANT TO EAGLES than their nesting sites are the areas where they gather in winter by the dozens or hundreds to catch fish during the day and roost by night in trees protected from icy northern blasts. Each autumn in Montana, for example, resource management agencies prohibit boating, walking, or driving within three miles downstream of the Canyon

An eagle in flight—the embodiment of elegance, strength, and nobility. FRANK OBERLE

Ferry Dam near Helena, where up to three hundred bald eagles gather to feed on spawned-out and dying kokanee salmon.

Another such oasis occurs at Keokuk, Iowa, where the mighty Mississippi churns through the hydro plant at Lock and Dam No. 19, masticating gizzard shad and remaining blessedly ice-free all winter. Eagles from Canada, Minnesota, and Wisconsin flock southward and park at Keokuk for the winter, sometimes four hundred strong, to dine on floating, headless shad and sleep in the welcoming trees of a nearby coulee on the Illinois shore.

The coulee is called Cedar Glen Eagle Roost. In 1979, The Nature Conservancy purchased nearly nine hundred acres to provide safe haven for wintering eagles—perhaps the first winter sanctuary established in the country. Since then several hundred additional acres have been purchased to protect the old hardwood roost trees from logging and provide protection from intrusive humans, including the thousands of eagle watchers that now flock to the area every winter. Humans must stay off the preserve from November through February when eagles are most numerous. After the birds go north, the Friends of Cedar Creek volunteer their time to tend to the trails and care for native vegetation.

The Conservancy and other organizations have worked with public agencies to protect other important roosting sites across the country:

One such area lies along the South Fork of the Snake River, where the stream spills from the deep folds of the Tetons into a wide valley of cottonwoods, Douglas fir, aspens, and wetlands. With abundant trout and thousands of wintering waterfowl, the sheltered canyon harbors the greatest concentration of nesting and wintering eagles in the greater Yellowstone region. Some residents saw a chance to cash in on the demand for homesites in this popular tourist area. One South Fork landowner even obtained the permits necessary to built sixty-six homes, a golf course, and a jet-boat marina. Outraged residents tried but failed to stop the development, so the Conservancy stepped in to buy land along twenty-five miles of the river to keep it wild. Federal agencies, groups such as the National Fish and Wildlife Foundation, and sympathetic individual buyers have joined in. Now about 90 percent of the river corridor is protected from further development.

In Wyoming, ranchers Oliver and Deborah Scott gave the Conservancy a conservation easement to protect seven thousand acres of prairie and woodland flanking the North Platte River where eagles roost and fish each winter.

Using great strength and mighty wings to reach the cold winter sky for the first hunt of the day. FRANK OBERLE

The Conservancy's Montana field office is working with the Confederated Salish and Kootenai Tribes of the Flathead Reservation to protect and manage a marshy bald eagle roost on the shores of Flathead Lake.

The National Wildlife Federation donated 150 acres along the Wisconsin River to protect wintering habitat in Wisconsin.

Along Washington's Skagit River, where several hundred eagles gather in winter to feed on spawned-out salmon, The Nature Conservancy negotiated with private landowners to increase the size of a state-owned preserve along the river. A proposal by the city of Seattle to build a hydroelectric project on the Skagit was quickly shelved after a study showed a dam and impoundment would diminish the salmon run and the eagles' winter food supply. Indeed, the Seattle utility has provided money to buy additional land and extend the preserve along the Skagit.

Farther south hundreds of wintering bald eagles congregate in the Klamath Basin, straddling the Oregon-California border. The Conservancy bought more than one thousand acres, which it sold to the U.S. Fish and Wildlife Service to include in the Bear Valley National Wildlife Refuge.

Nowhere else do bald eagles gather as they do along the coasts of British Columbia and southeastern Alaska. The granddaddy of all wintering refuges is the 48,000-acre Chilkat Bald Eagle Preserve near Haines, Alaska, where the state's panhandle meets the pan. As the Chilkat River approaches the Pacific, it spreads out in a broad flat. Ground-temperature water stored in the alluvial gravel seeps into the Chilkat, keeping it open all year. Up to three thousand eagles gather along the river, like rapacious fishermen wading into the shallows to snatch dying chum salmon drifting in the current. The state established the preserve in 1982 to protect the largest gathering of wintering bald eagles in existence. A small donation of land, made through The Nature Conservancy, added to extensive state holdings.

EVERY FALL THOUSANDS OF RAPTORS and other birds spill from the boreal forest of Canada and northern Minnesota and funnel along the northern shore of Lake Superior, aided in their migration by strong winds pushing them southward and by the thermals and updrafts lifting them above the rocky shore. Since the early 1950s, volunteers of the Duluth Audubon Society have gathered on Hawk Ridge, which rises above Superior's sparkling shore on the outskirts of town, to carefully count and tabulate the number of eagles and other large birds.

A mated pair of bald eagles. FRANK OBERLE

87

88

A nesting bald eagle at the Disney Wilderness Preserve in Florida. LYNDA RICHARDSON

A mature adult with a freshly caught kokanee salmon from the Missouri River in Montana. STEVE JUSTAD

During the '50s and '60s, the numbers of many raptors, including bald eagles, remained sparse. In 1953 and 1959, spotters saw no bald eagles at all. But beginning in about 1980, the numbers rose dramatically. In 1993, volunteers sighted 1,725, double the previous record.

No doubt about it, the bald eagle is back. During the past twenty years, its numbers have increased in every part of the continent. From Sandy Sprunt's count of fewer than 500 nesting pairs in 1963, the number of nesting pairs in the lower forty-eight states has increased to more than four thousand, according to the U.S. Fish and Wildlife Service. Counting juvenile birds, the number of bald eagles may total sixteen thousand. Alaskan and Canadian populations add several tens of thousands more.

The bald eagle is becoming so plentiful and widespread, it is even returning to nesting and roosting sites crowded by homes and offices.

"There has been a lot of education going on, with people learning to cohabit with these birds," says Joan Galli, ecologist with the nongame program for the Minnesota Department of Natural Resources. "You might be surprised that they would be so close to people."

Galli and I drive among the complex of lakes, marshes, and scattered woods just a few miles north of Minneapolis and St. Paul. Two decades ago, eagles were rarely seen in this part of the state. This year, about 20 pairs nest in the metropolitan area. "If you look at where they're nesting, it seems to me that for the most part they are still in islands of habitat that have a remoteness to them," Galli says. "From an eagle-eye perspective, those spots are pretty easy to find."

Galli stops the van, pulling fully onto the shoulder to avoid the steady traffic. She sets up a spotting scope on the gravel, turns it to a spreading white pine on the shore of a small lake, and stands aside so I can look. An adult eagle fidgets in a nest, shifting its weight from foot to foot. Suddenly the head of an eaglet pops up among the branches. "Eagles have learned a little adaptability, and people have learned to be tolerant of them and more courteous of them and more considerate," Galli says. In one instance, eagles have nested in a white pine growing in a suburban homeowner's backyard. Others nest in the flight path of planes using Minneapolis-St. Paul International Airport.

I recalled one spring when I walked along the Mississippi in the Katharine Ordway Natural History Study Area with David Clugston, who was then the resident naturalist. The private reserve borders River Lake, a backwater just downstream from the Twin Cities. "Just this year I found a

An eagle preparing to land and wait out a storm. FRANK OBERLE beaver lodge on the end of that peninsula and also some giant floater clams, which aren't supposed to be here because of the water quality," Clugston said. "Those are hopeful signs that the water quality is improving, but we have a long way to go." As he finished, I looked up to see a bald eagle soar into the branches of a tree by the river. Moments later, it was joined by another. All this fewer than ten miles from St. Paul.

For several years, that encounter stood as my quintessential urban eagle experience. But just the other day I glanced out my office window and noticed a bald eagle lazily flapping over downtown St. Paul, heading north with the other afternoon commuters on Interstate 35E.

BECAUSE THE EAGLE has fared so well, the U.S. Fish and Wildlife Service upgraded the bird's status in 1994 from endangered to threatened throughout the lower forty-eight states. The prognosis? "Right now it looks terrific," says Jody Millar, national recovery coordinator for the Fish and Wildlife Service in Rock Island, Illinois. "The eagle has made remarkable recovery since it was first protected."

The bald eagle is one of relatively few creatures on the endangered species list to show

Beginning a power dive to assert dominance over another eagle. FRANK OBERLE

92

improvement, much less hope of recovery. Others include the gray wolf and American alligator. More typical, however, are the California condor and Florida panther, which number so few their future is in grave doubt.

Why has the eagle fared relatively well, when other species have continued to slip deeper into the chasm of extinction?

First, the threat of DDT, though serious, was singular and relatively easy to eliminate. "To find one major causal agent is a blessing," says Millar. Far tougher than banning a single family of pesticides is attacking the multifarious problems of habitat destruction, competition from exotic species, and chronic poisoning by industrial contaminants—the combination that plagues many other species.

Second, bald eagles enjoyed a wide distribution and could adapt to a range of foods and habitats. Eliminating the birds from one area— such as much of the industrial East, Midwest, and South—didn't doom them. Eagles continued to thrive elsewhere on the continent.

Finally, it's easier to love a bald eagle than a dwarf wedge mussel or a Jessup's milk vetch. As fund-raisers of conservation groups know only too well, eagles, wolves, and whales speak to people. Conservationists even have a name for these glamour species: charismatic megafauna. And the eagle is nothing if not charismatic and mega.

What has the recovery of the bald eagle taught us about saving other endangered species? "I think there are lessons we can use, but they aren't simple lessons," says Deborah Jensen, Vice President and Director of Conservation Science and Stewardship for The Nature Conservancy.

First, "once decline was detected, people had to figure out why. That process can be used for any organism." The bald eagle might be nearing extinction today had we never discovered the connection between prolific use of DDT and nesting failure of eagles. Accurate population inventories and continuing scientific research are essential to detect problems, identify their causes, and develop solutions.

Designation of a species under the federal Endangered Species Act is vital. "It declares incontrovertibly that there is a problem," Jensen says. "Until that happens, then there is disagreement about whether or not a problem exists." Only with agreement come the resources and resolve necessary to remedy the problem.

Finally, says Jensen, "once a species is on the downward path, not all hope is lost. Recovery is possible. It will never be an easy fix, but that doesn't mean it isn't worth trying."

95

An early morning reflection in the Missouri River. STEVE JUSTAD

Heading back to roost at the close of another day. FRANK OBERLE

Hope inspires citizens to donate time, money, and effort. Hope produced the donations that set aside the James River National Wildlife Refuge. Hope drives National Wildlife Federation and Audubon volunteers into the cold and snow each winter to count wintering eagles. And it's hope that leads Jean Keene, a supervisor at a fish-packing plant who lives, quite literally, at the end of the road in Homer, Alaska, to set out fifty tons of freezer-burned fish for wintering birds. At times more than four hundred bald eagles gather behind her motor home. They occupy every available roost, and mill about with a rocking hunched-over gait, like stiff old men with wings, as they gulp down fish and the occasional intruding gull. "It gives them a helping hand during a tough time of the year," she says.

SCAVENGER AND FISH STEALER. Devoted mate for life, diligent parent, and hunter. We view our animals in moral terms. They are scoundrels or saints. Just as men create their gods, writes Barry Lopez in *Of Wolves and Men*, so do they also create their animals.

Not only does our severe anthropomorphism mislead us, it also blinds us to the eagle's exceptional adaptability. But if we insist on viewing the bald eagle in human terms, then I would offer this characterization from Stephen Fretwell in *The Bird Watch*. It hints at the complexity and utter suitability of the eagle to its environment. And Fretwell's remark, written as a fictional response of an eagle to a newspaper reporter, suggests also the reason the bald eagle is utterly suited to be our national symbol.

"The fellows who made me your symbol were more right than they knew," the eagle replies. "A fish dies and is washed up on shore. It looks bad and smells worse, is good for nothing, despised by all. I come and eat it and turn that fish … into a soaring wonder, a majestic greatness that stirs the heart of creatures everywhere, including men. Isn't that true for America, too? America was built by religious rejects, crooks, and poor people. All human waste, all looking bad and smelling worse, despised by all. This country consumed these people and … made them into a nation…. Like me, you … took the waste of the world and made something wonderful." ∞

Grace, power, and majesty. FRANK OBERLE

DIRECTORY OF BALD EAGLE VIEWING SITES

The following directory describes the best places to see wild bald eagles in the United States. Although eagles are likely to be seen at these areas during the recommended seasons, no sighting is guaranteed. Time and patience often are required to observe eagles, and many factors, including weather, influence the peak times of nesting, wintering, and migration. Eagle viewers should avoid disturbing birds, especially during nesting season. Maintain a reasonable distance, and use binoculars and spotting scopes for viewing.

ALABAMA

Lake Guntersville State Park

6,000-acre state park in NE corner of state. Best viewing: 50 to 60 bald eagles from Nov. through mid-Feb. or early Mar., 80 to 100 at peak in Jan. Eagle Awareness days in Jan.; awareness activities include driving tours around lake. From US 431, take AL 227 E about 7 miles to park entrance. Signs posted from US 431 direct visitors to park. Alabama Dept. of Conservation and Natural Resources, Div. of Parks. Contact: Lake Guntersville State Park Nature Center 205-571-5445.

Pickwick Lake

About 150 eagles congregate where the Tennessee River meets Pickwick Lake, in the NE corner of state near Tennessee and Mississippi. Best viewing: along a 7-mile stretch of the Tennessee River, 40 eagles may regularly be seen. By car from Florence, take County 14 NE about 25 miles to Water-loo. By boat, float from the Riverton area to the Natchez Trace Bridge. Eagles may also be seen from County 14, which follows the river for 2 miles before Waterloo. Land around Tennessee River owned by Tennessee Valley Authority. Contact: Alabama Nongame Wildlife Program 205-242-3867.

ALASKA

Alaska Chilkat Bald Eagle Preserve

48,000 acres of river bottomland of the Chilkat, Kleheni, and Tsirku rivers, NW of Juneau. The Chilkat Valley is home to 200 to 400 bald eagles year-round; 5 miles of open water on the Chilkat River allow eagles to fish when other waters are frozen. More than 80 eagle nests in the preserve. During winter months, early Oct. through Feb., more than 3,000 eagles may be seen in a small area. Best viewing: from Haines Hwy, miles 18 to 24. Managed by the Alaska Div. of Parks and Outdoor Recreation with the assistance of the Alaska Chilkat Bald Eagle Preserve Advisory Council. Contact: Alaska State Parks 907-465-4563; Haines Visitor Bureau 800-478-3579.

Steep Creek

Steep Creek flows from Heintzleman Ridge to Mendenhall Lake. Bald eagles concentrate along the lower mile of the creek (which flows through kettle ponds before reaching the lake) to feed on spawning cohos in Oct. and Nov. and often into Feb. Best viewing: from parking lot of the Mendenhall Glacier Visitor Center Observatory or from

Glacier Spur Rd., which parallels creek. Contact: USDA Forest Service, Juneau Ranger District 907-586-8800.

Stikine Flats Wildlife Viewing Area

As many as 1,500 bald eagles gather to feed on spawning eulachon in late Mar. to mid-May at Stikine Flats, at the mouth of the Stikine River in the Stikine-LeConte Wilderness Area, NW of Ketchikan. Look for them in the tall cottonwoods along the lower river and around pools and mudflats. Access by float plane or boat only. Viewing from boat or beaches. Contact: USDA Forest Service, Wrangell Ranger District 907-874-2323.

Alaska is believed to support a breeding population of at least 20,000 bald eagles. Probably half of that population is in coastal SE Alaska, where the birds are easy to see. Any time of the year, the Alaska Marine Highway ferry system and tour cruises along the coast provide visitors with good views of bald eagles. Driving the roads around Juneau, Ketchikan, Sitka, and Petersburg also affords views of eagles. Each community has its own nesting and year-round concentration of eagles, though eagles are most conspicuous during summer months. Contact: U.S. Fish and Wildlife Service 907-586-7243.

Other areas in Alaska with large breeding populations are Alaska Peninsula, Aleutian Islands, Bering Sea, Cook Inlet, interior Alaska, Kodiak and Afognak, and south-central Alaska. Most of these areas are not as accessible as the southeast coast, however, nor do they have as high a concentration of eagles.

ARIZONA

Becker Lake Wildlife Area

This 100-acre site is located mid-state, near the New Mexico line. Rimmed with cottonwood trees, it regularly attracts up to 5 or 6 wintering bald eagles from Dec. through Mar. From Springerville, take US 60/US 180 N 2.5 miles to entrance. Contact: Arizona Game & Fish Dept., Pinetop 602-367-4281.

Lake Mary

Both Upper and Lower Lake Mary, about 1,000 acres, provide good viewing of wintering bald eagles. Eagles may be seen Nov. through Apr., with peaks of 50 to 60 some winters. Best viewing: Oct. through Dec. along the paved highway that follows around the lakes at a higher elevation. On I-17 from Flagstaff, take exit 339. Go SE on Lake Mary Rd. (Forest Hwy. 3) for 5 miles to Lower Lake Mary and 9 miles to Upper Lake Mary. Contact: USDA Forest Service 602-556-7474.

Mormon Lake

Bald eagles usually winter at Arizona's largest lake (about 9 square miles) from Nov. through Apr.; counts reach 50 to 60 some winters. Best viewing: Oct. through Dec. at Doug Morrison Overlook, E side of lake. There is also a paved road around Mormon Lake. From Flagstaff, on I-17 at exit 339, take Lake Mary Rd. (Forest Hwy. 3) SE for 21 miles to Mormon Lake. Forest Rd. 90 circles around W side of the lake and returns to Forest Hwy. 3. Contact: USDA Forest Service 602-556-7474.

Nelson Reservoir

About 6 bald eagles spend the winter at this reservoir located on the Coronado Trail in SE Arizona near New Mexico. Typically, they arrive in Dec. and begin to migrate north in Mar. or Apr. The marshy area at the upper end of the reservoir, good waterfowl habitat, also attracts eagles. From Springerville, take US 191 (old US 666) E toward Alpine 8 miles. Contact: USDA Forest Service 206-333-4301.

ARKANSAS

Beaver Lake

On average, 150 to 200 bald eagles winter on this 31,700-acre lake in the NW corner of the state, a "Great Lake of the White River." Numbers peak in Jan. and Feb. Best viewing by boat (but by car too) between Rocky Branch Park and Dam Site Park, N part of lake. From Little Rock, travel W on I-40, N on AR 23, then W on AR 12. Contact: U.S. Army Corps of Engineers 501-636-1210.

Lake Greeson/Pike County

Lake Greeson is a 7,260-acre lake along the Little Missouri River N of Murfreesboro. Eagles winter here. Best viewing: by boat in Jan. and Feb. (one Jan., 122 eagles were counted). From Little Rock, travel S on I-30 to the Arkadelphia exit. Go W on AR 8, then W on US 70. Contact: U.S. Army Corps of Engineers 501-968-5008; Arkansas State Parks 501-682-2187.

The Arkansas Game & Fish Commission completes a mid-winter bald eagle survey each year. Contact Arkansas Game & Fish Commission for current best locations and counts, 2 Natural Resources Dr., Little Rock, AR 72205, 501-223-6300.

CALIFORNIA

Cache Creek

Wintering bald eagles populate a 25-mile stretch of Cache Creek (near Ukiah) mid-Nov. through Mar. As many as 60 eagles were counted one Jan.; the colder the weather, the greater the concentration. Good viewing near the North Fork of Cache Creek or from CA 16 along the creek. Guided hikes available in late Jan; reservations required. From Clearlake Oaks on CA 20 drive E 8 miles to entrance/parking area. Owners: California Dept. of Fish and Game, and Bureau of Land Management 707-468-4000.

Eagle Lake

Winter and breeding populations frequent this 28,000-acre lake in NE California. About 35 to 50 bald eagles stay Nov. through Mar. if the lake remains ice-free. Best viewing along 8 miles of CA 139 on the N shore of lake; also on S shore between Christy and Gallatin beaches. From Susanville follow CA 139 N 25 miles to Eagle Lake, or take County A-1 NW 16 miles to south part of lake. Contact: Bureau of Land Management 916-257-0456; USDA Forest Service 916-257-2151.

Lake San Antonio

From Nov. through Mar., more than 50 bald eagles roost in the shoreline snags of this 16-mile lake located between Monterey and San Luis Obispo. Best viewing: mid-Dec. through mid-Mar. from the Eagle Tour boat (birding information and binoculars provided). Reservation required; fee. At N edge of King City on US 101 take Jolon Rd./G-14 exit W for 24 miles. Turn right on Interlake Rd. for 12 miles, then right on San Antonio Rd. to the lake. Contact: Monterey County Water Resources Agency 805-472-2311.

Lewiston Lake and Trinity River Hatchery

In north-central California, 8 pairs of bald eagles nest in the area throughout the summer, some remaining all year. They feed on spawning salmon and steelhead. Best viewing from boat on lake or at fish hatchery. From Redding take CA 299 W 37 miles. Turn at sign to Trinity Dam/Lewiston Lake. At junction about 5.5 miles down, continue straight to Lewiston Lake or bear right to hatchery. Owned by California Dept. of Fish and Game, U.S. Bureau of Reclamation, and USDA Forest Service 916-623-2121.

Lower Klamath

This 46,902-acre refuge on the Oregon border is 1 of 6 in the Klamath Basin National Wildlife Refuge Complex. As many as 1,100 bald eagles winter here from Dec. into Mar., feeding on waterfowl and rodents. Good viewing along auto tour in refuge; look for eagles roosting in willows. From I-5 take US 97 N, then turn E on CA 161 for 9 miles to Lower Klamath auto tour. Contact: U.S. Fish and Wildlife Service 916-667-2231.

Silverwood Lake State Recreation Area

About 8 to 10 bald eagles, mature and immature, winter Dec. through Mar. in this 2,400-acre state park NE of Los Angeles. Park rangers and volunteers offer eagle boat tours Jan. through mid-Mar.; reservation required. Visitors may participate in mid-winter eagle counts. In Cajon Pass area on I-15 take CA 138 E for 12 miles to lake. Contact: California Dept. of Parks and Recreation 619-389-2303.

COLORADO

Alamosa National Wildlife Refuge

Two national wildlife refuges are part of this 14,189-acre complex in south-central Colorado above New Mexico. Staging bald eagles arrive during spring thaw around mid-Mar.; 40 to 100 eagles feed on exposed winter-killed fish from the Rio Grande. Good viewing from self-guided auto tour. Take US 160 E of Alamosa 3 miles or El Rancho Ln S of Alamosa 2 miles. Owned by U.S. Fish and Wildlife Service. Contact: Alamosa National Wildlife Refuge 710-589-4021.

Barr Lake State Park

2,609 acres of water and shore habitat just NE of Denver. A single pair of bald eagles remains in the park year-round and nests in the spring. Migrating eagles also show up occasionally. Birds can usually be viewed from hiking trails. Stop at nature center for viewing information. Nearest town is Brighton. Take I-76 E of Denver to exit 22, Bromley Ln. Go E on Bromley for 0.75 miles to Picadilly Rd. Turn right for 1.5 miles to park entrance; continue to nature center 303-659-6005.

Colorado River

Wintering bald eagles are often seen along US 550 between Montrose and Ouray and along the Colorado River, especially along Trough Rd. between Kremmling and State Bridge.

Jackson Lake State Park

2,800 acres of water and 400 of land, Jackson Lake is a major stopover for migrant bald eagles Mar. through May and Sept. through Oct. Good roadside viewing in and around park; look for eagles in cottonwoods near water. Between Jackson Lake and Denver, 48 pairs nest along the South Platte. Take I-76 NE of Denver, or US 34 E; signed exits lead to park. Contact: Colorado Div. of Parks and Outdoor Recreation 303-645-2551.

Rocky Mountain Arsenal

A 27-square-mile area just outside Denver, with 3,600 acres designated as the Rocky Mountain Arsenal Bald Eagle Management Area. From Nov. through Feb., a major winter roost on the E side of the wildlife area attracts 32 eagles which feed mostly on prairie dogs. The Eagle Watch, an observation point, overlooks the roost. Programs scheduled for visitors. To the Eagle Watch, take the Chambers Rd. exit N from I-70 to 56th St. Travel E on 56th to Buckley Rd. for 1.5 miles. Owned by the U.S. Army and U.S. Fish and Wildlife Service 303-289-0132.

CONNECTICUT

Connecticut River

Private companies offer guided boat tours on the Connecticut River for winter bald eagle viewing. Numbers peak at 30 eagles in Jan. The 100-foot Sunbeam Express offers a bald eagle boat tour in Jan. and Feb. leaving from Old Saybrook.

Shepaug Eagle Observation Area

Open water makes Shepaug Reservoirs and Dam, NE of Danbury, a wintering site for bald eagles. On average there are 8 to 10 eagles; sometimes there are none, sometimes, as many as 23. Reservations required; begin making them in mid-Dec. for weekends and Wednesdays throughout the winter. Guided viewing from blind with telescopes. Viewing possible through cooperative effort between Northeast Utilities, The Nature Conservancy, and the Connecticut Dept. of Environmental Protection. Property at dam and reservoir owned by Northeast Utilities 203-354-8840.

DELAWARE

Bombay Hook National Wildlife Refuge

On Delaware's Atlantic coast, a 15,978-acre refuge with 1 nesting pair of bald eagles year-round and some migrating immature birds. Best viewing: Nov. through Mar., when the leaves are off the trees in which the eagles nest, from along Shearness Rd., along Shearness Pool. Group tours available. Coming S on US 13, drive toward Smyrna. At the third stoplight in Smyrna, turn left onto Rd. 12. This will turn into DE 9. Drive S 0.25 miles more to sign for refuge. Turn left onto Rd. 85 and continue to visitor center. Contact: U.S. Fish and Wildlife Service 302-653-6872.

There are few nesting bald eagles in Delaware. Many of their nesting sites are on private land, or public access is closed. The sites are extremely sensitive.

FLORIDA

Big Bend Wildlife Management Area: Hickory Mound Impoundment

A 6.5-mile dike encircles this 1,834-acre management area SE of Tallahassee on the Gulf coast. Bald eagles stay here year-round, with largest concentrations during fall migration in Sept. and Oct. One active nest on Hickory Mound Impoundment and several in Taylor County; birds nest in Feb. and Mar. View of Impoundment nest from observation tower. On US 98, 18 miles W of Perry, turn W on Cow Creek Grade. Drive 6 miles on limerock road to check station for map and regulations summary. Contact: Florida Game and Fresh Water Fish Commission 904-838-1306.

Disney Wilderness Preserve

Over 11,000 acres of land 35 miles SW of Orlando. Currently not open to the public, a self-guided nature trail planned for the area around Lake Russell will allow public use by summer 1994. By fall 1995, a nature center will open. Bald eagles frequent the preserve year-round, with greatest numbers during winter nesting season. Of 20 active nests in the area, 6 are on the preserve. Owned and managed by The Nature Conservancy, Florida Region 407-935-0002.

Lake Kissimmee State Park

The bald eagle is just one of the rare species in this 5,030-acre park in central Florida, E of Tampa. Bald eagles can be seen year-round, with 3 active nests from Sept. through Apr. or May. Away from their nests, as many as a dozen eagles may be viewed from 13 miles of hiking trails or the observation tower. Restrictions apply during nesting season. From US 27 in Lake Wales, take FL 60 E 10 miles to Boy Scout Rd. Turn left for 3.7 miles. Turn right onto Camp Mack Rd. for 5.6 miles to park entrance. Dept. of Environmental Protection 813-696-1112.

Merritt Island National Wildlife Refuge

This 140,000-acre island on Florida's E coast shares a common boundary with Kennedy Space Center and Canaveral National Seashore. Bald eagles present late Aug. or Sept. through Mar. or Apr.; nesting begins late Nov. Numbers of pairs and individuals vary according to weather; few remain year-round. Good viewing along Black Point

Wildlife Drive by car; also, from observation tower, photo blind, and trails within the park. About 3.5 miles NE of Titusville. Take FL 406 out of Titusville onto FL 402. Refuge visitor center is on 402. Contact: U.S. Fish and Wildlife Service 407-861-0667.

Three Lakes Wildlife Management Area: Prairie Lakes Unit

This 8,203-acre management area S of Orlando contains Lakes Jackson, Kissimmee, and Marian. During winter nesting season, mid-Oct. through mid-May, there are 13 active nests. Eagles remain year-round, with greater numbers in winter. During nesting season some restrictions apply; please observe posted area around nests and stay at least 750 feet from nests. Good viewing from 5-mile hiking loop of the Florida Trail, or driving on Canoe Creek Rd. (FL 523). Future plans for a boardwalk and observation tower near Lake Marian. From Kenansville drive 9 miles NW on Canoe Creek Rd. Entrance on left (west). Contact: Florida Game and Fresh Water Fish Commission 407-436-1818.

GEORGIA

Specific site information is not available in Georgia due to small numbers and for reasons of protection. In general, eagles can be found along the coastal area and around the barrier islands.

IDAHO

Dworshak Reservoir

There are always 1 to 10 bald eagles in the immediate vicinity of Dworshak Reservoir, on the Clearwater River. Eagles winter here Nov. through Feb. Best viewing: along Ahsahka Rd. (road to powerhouse, which goes to base of dam). Walking trail along other side of dam. From below dam, watch eagles feeding on kokanee salmon. Near Orofino in N Idaho, at lower end of panhandle. From Orofino, cross Orofino Bridge and turn left on ID 7. Turn right just before Ahsahka Bridge and follow road to dam. Contact: U.S. Army Corps of Engineers 208-476-1255.

Lake Coeur d'Alene/Wolf Lodge Bay

This 900-acre bay attracts up to 60 migratory bald eagles when the kokanee salmon begin to spawn in Nov. Population peaks late Dec. to early Jan. Viewing from boat or car. Detailed brochure available. From Coeur d'Alene, take I-90 E 6 miles to Higgins Point; look for eagles from turn-out. Continue around bay on bridge over Wolf Lodge Creek at ID 97 junction. Contact: Bureau of Land Management, 1808 N. Third Street, Coeur d'Alene, ID 208-765-1511.

Silver Creek Preserve

In this 825-acre preserve 35 miles SE of Sun Valley, wintering bald eagles perch in trees and feed on waterfowl and fish in the creek's open spring-fed water. Good viewing Nov. through Feb.; about 10 eagles. Walk or cross-country ski to area of large cottonwood trees overlooking Sullivan's Lake. Directly off ID 20, 2 miles W of Picabo. Park and sign in at visitor center. Owner: The Nature Conservancy, Idaho Chapter 208-788-2203.

South Fork Snake River

25 of the 60 miles of the South Fork of the Snake River have a high-density, year-round bald eagle population. Considered part of the Greater Yellowstone Ecosystem bald eagle population, up to 200 birds may winter here. Best viewing: in summer, by boat. Complete brochure showing boat access available. The Nature Conservancy, Idaho Chapter; Bureau of Land Management; and USDA Forest Service own land along this stretch of river and work together on conservation efforts. Contact: Bureau of Land Management, Idaho Falls District 208-524-7500.

ILLINOIS

Cedar Glenn Eagle Roost

1,205 acres of varied habitat along the Mississippi River in W Illinois on the Iowa/Missouri border. In the coldest winters, more than 400 bald eagles have been counted. Peak viewing: Jan. and Feb., from areas near the preserve. (See Keokuk, Iowa, in this directory.) Closed to the public Nov. 1 to Mar. 1 for protection of the wintering eagles. The main road and bridge is IL 136. From the Illinois end of the bridge follow IL 136 E toward Hamilton. After 0.25 miles, turn S at the sign for Warsaw. The highway is not numbered, but is part of the Great River Road. The preserve is owned and managed by The Nature Conservancy, Illinois Field Office; Illinois Dept. of Conservation; and Western Illinois University. Contact: Kibbe Station resident manager 217-256-4519.

Crab Orchard National Wildlife Refuge

43,500 acres in S Illinois, near Carbondale. Dec. to Mar. viewing of about 20 bald eagles peaks in Jan. Two nesting pairs year-round. Car viewing only; organized car caravan tours available into restricted areas. Eagle weekends in late Jan. From I-57 exit 54b, 7 miles off exit. Owner: U.S. Fish and Wildlife Service. Contact: Crab Orchard National Wildlife Refuge 618-997-3344.

Lock and Dam 15/Quad Cities

Rock Island and Moline, Illinois, and Davenport and Bettendorf, Iowa, all along the Mississippi River, are the Quad Cities. During the winter, bald eagles feed on fish below the locks and dams where the water does not freeze over. From mid-Dec. through Feb., 60 to 70 eagles perch in wooded bluffs along or near the dam. Best viewing: from Fisherman's Corner Public Use Area, S entrance, Davenport riverfront, downstream of dam; Rock Island riverfront, downstream of dam; and Credit Island. Quad Cities Bald Eagle Days feature environmental exhibits, wildlife art, and eagle watching. Park ranger leads eagle watching weekends in Jan. Owner (lock sites): U.S. Army Corps of Engineers. Contacts: Mississippi River Visitor Center (on Arsenal Island) 309-794-5338; Quad Cities Visitor Bureau 800-747-7800.

INDIANA

Crane Division: Naval Surface Warfare Center

A 62,609-acre U.S. military base, including 820-acre Lake Greenwood, SW of Bloomington. 2 nesting pairs of bald eagles, 1 easily visible, present during summer. Peak viewing from mid-Mar. to May. Outdoor binoculars are set up to allow good views of eagle nest across lake. Special permission required to enter base; access granted 90% of the time. Weekday viewing preferred. Contact: Mr. Lynn Andrews, Natural Resources Manager 812-854-1165.

Monroe Lake

23,952 acres of land and water in S Indiana. Bald eagles present year-round; 2 nesting pairs on the lake late Feb. through summer. Greatest number present early Dec. through Mar., with peak (20 to 30) in Dec. Best viewing: from overlook areas around lake, boat launching area, or boat. If by boat, respect signed and buoyed restricted areas of the lake. One- to two-day eagle education program in Feb.; sign up early due to limited enrollment. Drive E from Bloomington on IN 46 and S on IN 446 about 6 miles to Paynetown Visitor Center. U.S. Army Corps of Engineers leases the Monroe Lake area to the Indiana Div. of Reservoir Management 812-837-9546.

Patoka Lake

In SW Indiana, Patoka Lake is 25 miles long with 161 miles of shoreline. Winter viewing of 8 to 10 eagles Oct.-Mar., peaking at 15 or more. Few eagles present year-round. Best viewing: Fisherman's Campground; upper beach parking lot; Newton-Stewart Ramp; marina; South Ramp; and Hwy. 145. Visitor center has printed material on local eagle viewing. From Jasper, turn N off IN 164 at Wicklife. Follow this road past gatehouse to visitor center. Owner: U.S. Army Corps of Engineers. Managed by Indiana Dept. of Natural Resources 812-685-2447.

IOWA

Keokuk Riverfront Area and Lock and Dam 19

Iowa, Illinois, and Missouri meet at Keokuk. From Nov. to Mar., up to 400 wintering bald eagles congregate in the largest area of open water on the Mississippi; numbers peak in Jan. Bald Eagle Appreciation Days in Jan.; indoor and outdoor activities. Owner (dam): Union Electric; (locks) U.S. Army Corps of Engineers. Contact: Keokuk Area Convention & Tourism Bureau, 401 Main St, Keokuk, 800-383-1219.

Lake Red Rock

Lake Red Rock, the largest lake in Iowa, is part of a 50,000-acre water and land base SE of Des Moines. Bald eagles congregate in Dec. and leave mid-Mar. Numbers peak in late Dec. and early Jan. with 20 to 30 below the dam when the lake freezes. The U.S. Army Corps of Engineers holds Eagle Watches in late Feb. or early Mar. in nearby Pella. The local raptor center offers educational programs including live raptors indoors. Biologists and rangers set up spotting scopes on the bridge for public viewing of the eagles across the Des Moines River. General winter viewing along river, near campground, and from bike trail. From Pella, take T-15 S for 4 miles to Red Rock Dam. Contact: U.S. Army Corps of Engineers Visitor Center (at S end of dam) 515-828-7522.

Also see Lock and Dam 15/Quad Cities area (in Illinois listings).

KANSAS

John Redman Dam and Reservoir

The reservoir, with a 59-mile shoreline, lies in a broad valley in the Flint Hills region S of Topeka. An average of 60 wintering bald eagles Oct. through Mar., with numbers in Jan. and Feb. peaking at 120. Best viewing: from upstream side of dam and around shoreline; also from town of Ottumwo at Hickory Creek. Both areas accessible by car. Walking trail and observation tower at Doves Roost (W of Kennedy Creek, N side of lake). The local Audubon chapter sponsors an Eagle Tour in Jan.; call in Dec. for dates. On the Neosho River about 3 miles N and 1 mile W of Burlington, just off US 75. Contact: U.S. Army Corps of Engineers 316-364-8613.

Perry Reservoir

Wintering bald eagles can be seen Nov. through early Mar. around this 11,500-acre lake, with about 200 birds in Jan. Most viewing from car. From Topeka, drive E on US 24 about 15 miles. Turn N at Perry for 3 miles. Owner: U.S. Army Corps of Engineers. Contact: Perry Reservoir Information Center 913-597-5144.

Riverfront Plaza, Lawrence

A three-story shopping mall between Kansas City and Topeka with one-way glass windows looking across the Kansas River. Consistent viewing of 10 to 20 bald eagles from inside mall Dec. through Feb. Public not allowed on promenade in winter months. Take I-70 to exit 204 (East Lawrence). Travel S 1 mile over bridge, turn left and drive one block to corner of 6th and New Hampshire. Owner (mall): Chelsea GCA Realty. Contact: Riverfront Plaza Information 800-913-4567.

KENTUCKY

Ballard Wildlife Management Area

8,373 acres including 11 oxbow lakes, in W Kentucky. 3 nesting pairs of bald eagles summer through fall. Viewing from 1-mile loop in car or on foot. From Paducah, travel US 60 W 17 miles to LaCenter. Take KY 358 for 5.6 miles to KY 473 into Bandana. Take KY 1105 6 miles to KY 473 again. Turn left off 473 at Lodge Rd for 1 mile to entrance. Contact: Kentucky Dept. of Fish and Wildlife Resources 502-224-2244.

Land Between the Lakes

See Land Between the Lakes in Tennessee section. To N entrance: From I-24, go 5 miles S on KY 453 through Grand Rivers.

LOUISIANA

White Kitchen Preserve

A freshwater marsh and cypress swamp preserve. From Sept. to May, a single nesting pair of bald eagles at site that has been occupied for at least 80 to 90 years. Site visible from the end of the Chevron Boardwalk. Best viewing: Feb. and Mar. Self-guiding tour brochure available at local stores and restaurants or from Louisiana Field Office of The Nature Conservancy. The short boardwalk begins at State of Lousiana rest area at junction of US 190 and US 90 near southern Louisiana/Mississippi border. Contact: The Nature Conservancy 504-338-1040.

MAINE

Acadia National Park

This 34,370-acre national park S of Bangor has both inland and coastal habitat. Bald eagles year-round in and around the park, with several nest sites. Nesting eagles arrive late Feb. and Mar. and fledge in early Jul. Best viewing: June through Aug. with private water-based tours often accompanied by naturalists. Park visitor center open May 1 to Oct 31. Take ME 3 to Mt. Desert Island and follow signs. Park headquarters, off ME 233, open in winter. Contact: National Park Service 207-288-3338.

Cobscook Bay State Park/Moosehorn National Wildlife Refuge

The state park, on Cobscook Bay on Maine's northernmost coast, and the refuge, adjacent and inland from the park, boast the state's highest density of nesting bald eagles. Some remain year-round. Several nesting pairs visible Mar. through Aug., with 3 to 4 pairs right on the bay and 1 often visible from US 1. Magurrewock Marsh in Baring Unit of refuge also a good spot for viewing. To reach the park take US 1 E from Machias through Whiting. Signs for park posted on E side of 1. Contact: Maine Bureau of Parks and Recreation 207-726-4412. For refuge, take ME 9 to US 1 through Baring to entrance on S side of 1. Contact: U.S. Fish and Wildlife Service 207-454-7161.

Holbrook Island Sanctuary

This 1,250-acre preserve W of Acadia National Park includes both freshwater ponds and saltwater shoreline. Pairs of mature bald eagles year-round, with 2 to 3 nesting sites in the park. Viewing from car, using car as a blind, and from trails, some along shoreline. Day use only. From ME 176 look for Cape Rosier Rd. on W side. Follow signs to park. Contact: Maine Bureau of Parks and Recreation 207-326-4012.

Howard Mendall Wildlife Management Area

A 370-acre area of mostly wetland with some upland area SW of Bangor. Bald eagles year-round, with single nesting pair Mar. through Aug. Best viewing of wintering eagles: Dec. through Feb. from mouth of marsh near entrance. No established trails. Follow ME 1A S from Frankfort. Just after boat launch area look for signs for management area 0.5 miles farther on left. Contact: Maine Dept. of Inland Fisheries & Wildlife 207-547-4165.

Steve Powell Wildlife Management Area/Swan Island

A 1,755-acre management area comprised of two islands on the Kennebec River between Augusta and Brunswick. 1 nesting pair of bald eagles on one island and 2 to 3 nests in vicinity. Best viewing early May through Labor Day along the Kennebec and on islands, by canoe or on trails; reservation required. Interpretational tours available. Parking area and boat landing in Richmond on river bank. Contact: Maine Dept. of Inland Fisheries & Wildlife 207-547-4167.

The Maine Chapter of The Nature Conservancy (207-729-5181) currently owns 17 preserves protecting bald eagle habitat in Maine. These sites are protected by The Nature Conservancy in part because the eagles are particularly sensitive to disturbance. The sites are not open to the public during the nesting season. The Nature Conservacy's Maine Chapter is also involved in cooperative bald eagle protection projects with such groups as the U.S. Fish & Wildlife Service, Maine Dept. of Inland Fisheries & Wildlife, and Land for Maine's Future Board. In Maine the bald eagle status is still considered to be in need of protection.

MARYLAND

Blackwater National Wildlife Refuge

Over 20,000 acres supporting several different species 12 miles S of Cambridge on the Eastern Shore, Chesapeake Bay. About 60 bald eagles present year-round. Almost 29 active nests in the spring; winter populations often exceed 100. Drive, walk, or bike self-guided tour in western portion of refuge for views of eagles in tall loblolly pines; get tour brochure at visitor center. Contact: U.S. Fish and Wildlife Service 410-228-2677.

Aberdeen Proving Grounds, Blackwater National Wildlife Refuge, Pocomoke, Hopewell, Rappahannock, Caledon State Park, and Mason Neck National Wildlife Refuge are all eagle concentration areas on Chesapeake Bay. Blackwater National Wildlife Refuge is probably the best of these sites. Contact: U.S. Fish and Wildlife Service in Annapolis 301-269-5448.

Conowingo Dam

From mid-Nov. through Jan., bald eagles congregate on the open water of the Lower Susquehanna River above and below Conowingo Dam. Peak numbers of eagles in Dec. perch in trees on both sides of river. Nesting pairs in Conowingo Recreation Project area; some migrants in Aug. Viewing platform at Conowingo Fishermen's Park and Boat Launch below dam, about 0.5 miles from parking area; viewing of up to 40 eagles per day. Eagle watching programs in Nov. and Dec.; educational programs available through visitor center. On US 1 just S of Pennsylvania in NE Maryland. Contact: Conowingo Recreation Project, Philadelphia Electric Co. 410-457-5011.

MASSACHUSETTS

Barton Cove

A single nesting pair of bald eagles occupies Barton Island, in the Connecticut River N of Northampton, from Mar. through Aug., becoming more active late Mar. through Jul. Best viewing: from public boat ramp off MA 2, or just E of boat ramp at Barton Cove Nature and Camping Area. Boating prohibited in immediate area surrounding Barton Island and nest. Both boat ramp and nature area in Gill just off MA 2. From I-91, follow MA 2 E through Greenfield to first stoplight in Gill. Follow signs for boat ramp. Owner: Northeast

Utilities. Contact: Northfield Mountain Environmental Center 413-659-3714.

Quabbin Reservoir

25,000 acres of water and 120,000 of watershed E of Northampton. From Dec. to Mar., 20 to 50 eagles; peak in Feb. Best viewing: from Endfield Lookout; viewing by boat not recommended. Off MA 9 between Ware and Belchertown. Owner: Massachusetts Metropolitan District Commission. Contact: visitor center 413-323-7221.

MICHIGAN

Erie Marsh

Migrating bald eagles can be seen in this preserve, one of many marshes along Lake Erie in SE Michigan. Best viewing: Mar., Apr., and early fall, from trails throughout preserve; watch for roosting and flying eagles. Closed for duck-hunting season mid-Sept. through Nov. From Monroe take I-75 S to exit 2 (Summit Rd). Go SE on Summit to Stearns Rd. Make a U-turn and head back N/NE on Bay Creek Rd 0.8 miles to Dean Rd. Turn E on Dean Creek for 1 mile. Park at the Erie Shooting Club Cottages. Owner: The Nature Conservancy, Michigan Field Office 517-332-1741.

Presque Isle Flowage

800 acres of bottomlands in the western Upper Peninsula. One nesting pair of bald eagles active from May through Oct. Best viewing: from boat. About 2.5 miles S of Marenisco on MI 64. Entrance W side of road. Contact: USDA Forest Service 906-667-0261.

Seney National Wildlife Refuge

A 95,455-acre wildlife refuge in the middle of the Upper Peninsula, in Schoolcraft County. 3 pairs of bald eagles nest and several immature eagles summer on the refuge. Best viewing: Feb./Mar. to late Oct., when ice forms, from 7-mile

Marshland Wildlife Drive self-guided tour. Eagle nest observation deck with spotting scope and interpretive panel located along drive. Visitor center open May 15 to Oct. 15. 3 entry points to refuge: entrance road off MI 77, 2 miles N of Germfask; Driggs River Rd. off MI 28; and at cross-country ski area off MI 77, S of Germfask. Contact: U.S. Fish and Wildlife Service 906-586-9851.

MINNESOTA

Chippewa National Forest

900 miles of rivers and 1,321 acres of lakes. Occasional migrating and wintering bald eagles, but frequent summer nesting pairs, with count in 1993 of 186. Best viewing: mid-Mar. through Nov., by canoe on Mississippi River between Cass Lake and Lake Winnie; also, by Leech Lake Dam and Winnie Dam, and any large lakes and rivers. View from boat, walking along shores, and at campgrounds, picnic areas, and boat landings. Educational programs at individual visitor centers in forest. S entrance about 200 miles N of Twin Cities. Contact: USDA Forest Service 218-335-8600.

Lac qui Parle Wildlife Refuge and Management Area

During Nov. and Dec., about 60 immature bald eagles congregate in the 32,000-acre refuge and management area near Milan in Chippewa County. One nest site on refuge visible to public; eagles remain throughout the winter. Best viewing: along the 1.5-mile stretch of County 32 after junction with County 13, and from other roads along the refuge N of dam or near Lac qui Parle Lake. Contact: Minnesota Dept. of Natural Resources 612-734-4451.

Red Wing area of the Mississippi River

From Nov. through Mar., Colvill Park and Bay Point Park in Red Wing, 55 miles SE of the Twin Cities, attract concentrations of wintering eagles. Numbers peak in Dec. Best viewing: Bay Point Park and Colvill Park waterfronts.

111

Located 55 miles S of the Twin Cities. Follow MN 61 W to Red Wing. Watch for signs to waterfront parks. Contact: Wisconsin Dept. of Natural Resources, Nongame Wildlife Program 612-296-3344.

Sherburne National Wildlife Refuge

This refuge on the Saint Francis River just NW of the Twin Cities is year-round habitat for some bald eagles, with at least 2 nesting pairs Apr. through Aug. Peak viewing of nesting pairs May to Jun. from observation decks with telescopes located along 8-mile wildlife drive. Visitor centers offer educational programs for groups. From I-94, take MN 101 from Rogers to Elk River, where road becomes US 169. Go N on 169 about 20 miles, then W on County 9 for 4 miles to entrance. Contact: U.S. Fish and Wildlife Service 612-389-3323.

Tamarac National Wildlife Refuge

This 43,000-acre refuge E of Fargo, North Dakota, has 17 active bald eagle nests, with more on lands near refuge. A few eagles remain year-round with high numbers in spring and summer, peaking at about 90 during migration in Oct. and Nov. Best viewing: from County 26 on refuge boundary; on walking trails within refuge near water; and from auto tour route. Located 18 miles NW of Detroit Lakes off County 29 and 26. Owner: U.S. Fish and Wildlife Service. Contact: Tamarac National Wildlife Refuge Visitor Center 218-847-2641.

Voyageurs National Park

There are normally 33 nesting pairs of bald eagles around both Rainy and Kabetogama lakes and islands. Eagles remain year-round, fishing in open water and feeding off road and wolf kills. In spring, when ice breaks up in Black Bay near Rainy Lake, as many as 120 eagles feed on fish. Best viewing: from boat; guided tours offered. Leave car at visitor centers. Naturalist-guided programs part of evening campfire activities. To Rainy Lake, drive 12 miles E of

International Falls on MN 11. To Kabetogama Lake, take US 53, then MN 122 four miles to visitor center. Contact: National Park Service 218-283-9821.

Wabasha area of the Mississippi River

From Nov. to Mar., 50 to 75 bald eagles feed at Wabasha, about 115 miles SE of the Twin Cities, where the Chippewa River flows into the Mississippi and creates ice-free water all winter. Best viewing: from road pullouts between Camp Lacupolis and Read's Landing, at Read's Landing, and in Wabasha along Lawrence Blvd. Volunteers at viewing platform 1 to 3 pm Sundays from early Nov. through Mar. 29. Special group talks and guided sessions available. Drive S on MN 61. Contact: Wabasha Chamber of Commerce 612-565-4158.

In the past, the Minnesota Chapter of The Nature Conservancy has acquired land and transferred it to federal and state agencies to manage as wildlife habitat. Some of this land forms what is now Chippewa National Forest, Lac qui Parle Wildlife Refuge and Management Area, and Voyageurs National Park.

MISSISSIPPI

Currently, Mississippi has no sites for public viewing of bald eagles, but eagles may be seen near inland lakes and reservoirs throughout the state. No large winter concentrations at this time. Contact: Mississippi Dept. of Wildlife, Fisheries and Parks 601-362-9212.

MISSOURI

Sandy Island Natural History Area

From 50 to 200 bald eagles spend part of their winter

from Dec. to Mar. in this 25-acre area near Lock and Dam 25/Winfield Dam on the Mississippi River. Currently closed to the public, the area will have an eagle viewing platform by fall 1994 through a cooperative effort of The Nature Conservancy, U.S. Army Corps of Engineers, and Union Electric. Off MO 79 about 40 minutes N of St. Louis. Contact: The Nature Conservancy, Missouri Chapter 314-968-1105.

The Missouri Dept. of Conservation hosts Eagle Days, a 2-day event, in Dec. and Jan., including indoor educational programs with a live bald eagle and guided outdoor viewing. Eagle Days rotate among Clarksville, Lake of the Ozarks/Bagnell Dam, Mingo National Wildlife Refuge, Squaw Creek/Mound City, and Table Rock Lake. Contact: Missouri Dept. of Conservation 314-751-4115 ext. 194.

MONTANA

Fort Peck Dam

40 or more wintering bald eagles congregate on open water below dam from Nov. through late Feb. or Mar. Best viewing: near dam, from Roundhouse Point; watching the birds on the ice shelves; and from gravel and dirt roads below power plants. In NE Montana. Off MT 117 below Fort Peck power plants. Contact: U.S. Army Corps of Engineers 406-526-3411.

Gates of the Mountains

On Holter Lake; boat access only. About 25 breeding and nonbreeding bald eagles summer in this area; immature and young birds that fledge in early Jul. increase total numbers. Gates of the Mountains boat tour offers 2-hour cruise for fee. Private boats pay launch fee. Private visitor center/display at boat launch. From Helena drive 20 miles N on I-15 to Gates of the Mountains exit. Continue 2.8 miles to Gates of the Mountains boat tour and public boat launch. Contact: 406-458-5241.

Hauser Lake

From mid-Oct. to early Dec., over 300 eagles feed on spawning kokanee salmon below Canyon Ferry Dam on the Missouri River. Best viewing: from Riverside Campground immediately below the dam at headwaters of Hauser Lake. Visitor center in Canyon Ferry Village at N end of reservoir open during summer and fall migration period. From Helena, take Canyon Ferry Rd. over the dam to campground. Eagle viewing signs posted. The Bureau of Reclamation manages the site in cooperation with the Montana Bald Eagle Working Group, including Montana Dept. of Fish, Wildlife & Parks, Montana State Parks and Wildlife Interpretive Association, U.S. Army Corps of Engineers, USDA Forest Service, Bureau of Land Management, Montana Power Co., Montana State University, and the Helena Chamber of Commerce. Contact: 406-475-3319.

Kootenai River/Libby Dam

25 to over 100 bald eagles winter below Libby Dam on the Kootenai River in NW Montana. Numbers peak Dec./Jan. Best viewing: from roads along the river and from Alexander Creek Picnic Area. Visitor center on Forest Service Rd. 228. From Libby go N on MT 37 13.5 miles to FSR 228, just before bridge over Kootenai River. Take FSR 228 to Powerhouse Rd. Contact: U.S. Army Corps of Engineers 406-293-5577.

Lee Metcalf National Wildlife Refuge

From a few to 20 bald eagles frequent this site on the Bitterroot River winter through Mar. Picnic area, 140 acres, open year-round for walking and wildlife viewing. Take US 93 to Stevensville. Turn E on Eastside Hwy. Turn on Wildfowl Ln for 1.5 miles; watch for refuge boundary signs. Contact: U.S. Fish and Wildlife Service 406-777-5552.

Rocky Mountain Front

More than 100 bald eagles migrate through this area on the eastern front of the Rocky Mountains mid-Feb. to mid-Apr., with highest numbers in Mar. (Numbers even higher for golden eagles.) Best viewing: from Bowmans Corners to Rogers Pass; find vantage point along MT 200. From Lincoln, go E on MT 200 15 miles to top of Rogers Pass. Continue E to Bowmans Corners at junction of 200 and US 287. Contact: USDA Forest Service 406-362-4265.

NEBRASKA

Johnson 2 Hydro Plant

From mid-Dec. to about Mar., typically 40 bald eagles congregate on the open water near this hydro plant on the Tri-County Supply Canal in south-central Nebraska. Plant provides spotting scopes and bleachers before viewing windows. From I-80 take Lexington exit S onto US 283. Past truck stop, go left on blacktop canyon road for 3 miles S, 1 mile E, and 1 mile S again over supply canal. Turn W (right) onto unmarked county road and continue to plant. Contact: Central Nebraska Public Power & Irrigation District 308-995-8601.

Kingsley Dam

From 15 to 350 wintering eagles gather at Lake Ogallala, a small lake below dam, to feast on dead fish from hydro plant. Water stays open when nearby waters freeze. Mid-Dec. through Mar.; numbers peak Jan./Feb. Small heated trailer with large bay windows available for viewing. From I-80, exit at O'gallala. Go N through town and follow signs for Lake McConaughy and Kingsley Dam. Contact: Central Nebraska Public Power and Irrigation District 308-284-2332.

NEVADA

Lahontan State Recreation Area

Upper and Lower Lahontan Reservoirs, 17 miles long with a total of 69 miles of shoreline, are located on Carson River. From 1 to 10 wintering bald eagles may be seen here from Nov. through Mar. View by driving or walking around lake. Look in trees along shoreline. Located 50 miles E of Carson City off NV 50 or 20 miles SW of Fallon off NV 50. Part of the Newlands Water Project; owned by State of Nevada, Div. of State Parks. Contact: 702-867-3001.

Lake Mead National Recreation Area

This 1.5 million-acre recreation area comprises both Lake Mead, formed by Hoover Dam; and Lake Mohave, formed behind Davis Dam; and the land surrounding these lakes. This is a wintering area for bald eagles from late Nov. through Apr. Based on annual winter eagle surveys, the typical number of eagles that winter in the area is 20. Substantially higher numbers have been counted in recent years. Best viewing is by boating on either lake, specifically the Cottonwood Grove area on Lake Mohave and the Overton Arm on Lake Mead. Also, driving the Northshore Rd. within the recreation area. Located in the southern tip of Nevada, 25 miles SE of Las Vegas. Access off US 93/95 from Las Vegas or off I-15 at the N end of the recreation area. Owner: National Park Service 702-293-8906.

Ruby Lake National Wildlife Refuge

37,600-acre refuge system of marshes. From 1 to 4 eagles may be seen on the refuge Nov. through Feb. A single eagle normally perches in a large tree near the historical site of Bressman Cabin on County 767. More viewing from diked roads throughout marsh system. From Elko take Jiggs Hwy. (NV 228). Travel 3 miles beyond Jiggs and turn left onto Harrison Pass Summit Rd. Turn right onto County 767, also called Ruby Lake Valley Rd. This road sometimes closes in winter; call ahead for information. The refuge headquarters is 9 miles down this road. Owner: U.S. Fish & Wildlife Service 702-779-2237.

Stillwater National Wildlife Refuge

This 77,000-acre refuge is a wintering area for bald eagles. Around 5 to 10 bald eagles may be in the area from late Nov. through Mar. Best viewing: late Dec. when eagles often sit out on ice. Drive roads throughout refuge and look for eagles near units that currently have open water. Located 15 miles east of Fallon off NV 50. Owner: U.S. Fish & Wildlife Service 702-423-5128.

NEW HAMPSHIRE

Adam's Point Wildlife Management Area

5 to 15 bald eagles winter in these 4,500 acres of tidal water and wetland and 800 acres of coastal land in New Hampshire's Great Bay area. Best viewing: late Nov./early Dec. to Mar., from walking trail leading onto point; look for eagles along open water. Access trail from University of New Hampshire Jackson Lab parking lot. From Durham, take NH 108 toward Newmarket; after Oyster River, take first left on Durham Point Rd. about 3 miles until fence and sign for lab; road to parking lot through opening in fence. Owner: New Hampshire Fish and Game Dept. 603-271-2462. Also contact Audubon Society of New Hampshire 603-224-9909.

In general, bald eagles winter along major rivers throughout New Hampshire. Much of the land along the rivers is privately owned and not accessible to the public at this time.

NEW JERSEY

Delaware Water Gap National Recreation Area

Bald eagles winter in the upper Delaware River region, between East Stroudsburg and Port Jervis. 10 to 20 birds visible. Best viewing: from Delaware River bridges and river roads in New Jersey and Pennsylvania in Jan. and Feb., with peak in Jan. Boat access possible. Water Gap managed by National Park Service, but associated areas along river mostly privately owned. Remain on public roads and lands. Contact: 717-296-6952.

Dividing Creek

From 1 to 8 bald eagles winter in the area of the marsh at Maple St, just W of the town of Dividing Creek in southernmost New Jersey. Jan. to Feb.; periodically, subadult eagles also in area June through Aug. Best viewing: from car; stop along road. From Millville, take County 555 to County 553 into Dividing Creek. Owners: New Jersey Div. of Fish, Game and Wildlife and Philadelphia Conservationists, Natural Lands Trust (private conservation organization). Contact: Endangered and Nongame Species Program, New Jersey Div. of Fish, Game and Wildlife 609-628-2436.

Forsythe National Wildlife Refuge, Brigantine Unit

From 1 to 5 bald eagles winter in this area N of Atlantic City Jan. through Feb.; peak in Jan. Best viewing: from 8-mile auto tour around 2 impoundments adjacent to a salt marsh. Interpretive displays at visitor center. Take exit 41 off Garden State Pkwy, then Jim Leeds Rd or Creek Rd E to State Rt 9. Entrance E of Rt 9 in Oceanville. Contact: U.S. Fish and Wildlife Service 609-652-1665.

Maurice River/Delaware Bay

Bald eagles winter at this site in Cumberland County Dec. through Feb., peaking at 10 to 20 in Jan. Access points from NJ 47 just S of NJ 55 include Mauricetown Bridge near Mauricetown, and roads from Port Elizabeth, Dorchester, and Leesburg, which end at river. Some viewing from Delaware Bay beaches, including Moore's Beach (off Alt. Rt 47 on Moore's Beach Rd). Private ownership of land along road; do not trespass. Contact: Endangered and Nongame Species Program, New Jersey Div. of Fish, Game and Wildlife 609-628-2436.

Stow Creek Bald Eagle Nest

A single pair of bald eagles nests in Canton on the border of Salem and Cumberland counties Feb. to early Aug. Remain on roads; no access allowed in fields or private land. Viewing area proposed for site for summer 1994. Access via NJ 49 and county road from Salem. Contact: Endangered and Nongame Species Program, New Jersey Div. of Fish, Game and Wildlife 609-628-2436.

NEW MEXICO

Conchas Reservoir

From Nov. through Feb., about 40 bald eagles winter on this 25-mile-long, 9,600-acre reservoir NW of Tucumcari in east-central New Mexico. Best viewing: from boat; lake's many arms and limited road access make roadside and shore viewing unsuccessful. On NM 104, head for settlement of Conchas until you reach the reservoir. Limited roads to SE and south-central areas of lake. Owner: U.S. Army Corps of Engineers. Contact: Conchas Lake State Park 505-868-2270.

Elephant Butte Lake State Park

A peak number of 80 bald eagles (in Jan.) winter on this 36,500-acre, 43-mile-long lake S of Albuquerque. Best viewing: Nov. through Mar. by boat and from dirt roads. 7 miles N of Truth or Consequences on I-25. Contact: New Mexico Park and Recreation Div. 505-744-5421.

McAllister Lake/Las Vegas National Wildlife Refuge

These adjoining areas NE of Albuquerque provide habitat for migrating waterfowl and about 25 wintering bald eagles from Nov. through Mar. McAllister Lake open year-round; the refuge is less accessible. Viewing from car or on foot. From I-25 at S edge of Las Vegas, turn E on NM 104 1.2 miles. Turn S (right) on NM 281 4 miles to refuge office, another 0.5 miles to Crane Lake Overlook, and 3 more miles to McAllister Lake. Contact: (McAllister Lake) New Mexico

Dept. of Game and Fish 505-445-2311; (Refuge) U.S. Fish and Wildlife Service 505-425-3581.

Maxwell Lake National Wildlife Refuge

The refuge and its three lakes are on the migration corridor on the front range of the Rocky Mountains. From Nov. through Mar. in recent winters, the middle lake, Lake 13, has offered views of almost 40 bald eagles. In NE corner of state. Exit I-25 at mile marker 426 and go W 2 blocks into Maxwell. Go 0.75 miles N on NM 445, then W on NM 505 2.5 miles to entrance. Headquarters 1.25 miles N. Contact: U.S. Fish and Wildlife Service 505-375-2331.

Navajo Reservoir

From Nov. through Feb., about 42 bald eagles winter on this 15,000-acre lake in the NW corner of the state, E of Farmington. Best viewing: because of hundreds of miles of shoreline, from boat. 25 miles E of Bloomfield on US 64 and NM 511. Owner: Bureau of Reclamation. Contact: Navajo State Park 505-632-2278.

Ute Reservoir

With 8,200 acres, many arms and inlets, and little road access, Ute Reservoir provides safe winter haven for about 45 bald eagles from Nov. through Feb. Best viewing: from boat. NE of Tucumcari (near Texas border), 3 miles W of Logan via NM 540. Land leased by New Mexico State Parks. Contact: Ute Lake State Park 505-487-2284.

El Vado and Heron Reservoirs

The surfaces of these twin lakes near the Colorado border, N of Santa Fe, cover 5,900 acres. 20 bald eagles Nov. through Feb. Best viewing: from boat; limited access from shorelines. Go 14 miles SW of Tierra Amarilla on NM 112 to El Vado. Drive 11 miles W of Tierra Amarilla on US 64 and NM 95 to Heron. State parks at each reservoir. Owner: Bureau of Reclamation. Contact: Heron Lake State Park 505-588-7470.

NEW YORK

Iroquois National Wildlife Refuge

There is a single active nesting pair on this 10,818-acre refuge that is visable from the refuge headquarters. Best viewing of nesting is during Apr., May, and June. Observation cameras have been set up so that visitors may view the nesting eagles from the headquarters without disturbing the eagles. N of Batavia off of NY 63 (in town of Alabama). Owner: U.S. Fish & Wildlife Service 716-948-5445.

Montezuma National Wildlife Refuge

This 6,485-acre refuge in central New York state offers a public observation platform that allows close-up views of a nesting pair of bald eagles. Maps and brochures are available at the visitors center, staffed part time. Located 40 minutes west of Syracuse right off the New York State Thruway (I-90). Owner: U.S. Fish & Wildlife Service 315-568-5987.

St. Lawrence River

The stretch of the St. Lawrence River along the New York-Canada border is a wintering spot for bald eagles. 6 to 12 eagles use the open water on this portion of the river from early Dec. through mid-Mar. Best viewing: from auto along NY 12 on U.S. side of river; from Rt. 401 on Canada side. Peak viewing from Jan. 1 through Feb. 20. Look for areas of open water or gull and waterfowl concentrations along river—including Chippewa Bay, Wellesley Island, Ivy Lea, and Brockville Narrows areas. Drive at the southern end of the river near the Thousand Islands Bridge and continue E to Massena and Robert Moses State Park. Contact: New York State Dept. of Environmental Conservation, Wildlife Office, 317 Washington St., Waterton, NY 13601, 315-785-2261.

Sullivan County

A wintering area for up to 50 eagles from early Dec. through Mar. Best viewing: Jan. 1 through Feb. 20 from Rio Reservoir or Monguap Falls Reservoir, and the Upper Delaware River. View from public roads around both reservoirs and from NY 97 along Delaware River. Located in southern New York south of the Catskill Mountains. Land in area owned by Orange and Rockland Utilities Corporation, New York State Dept of Environmental Conservation, and private. Contact: New York State Dept. of Environmental Conservation, Endangered Species Unit, Wildlife Resources Center, Game Farm Rd, Delmar, NY 12054, 518-439-7635.

NORTH CAROLINA

Jordan Lake

A reservoir of the Haw River. As many as 60 bald eagles roost and feed here from May through Aug. Observation deck/viewing platform. Principal access from US 64 causeway over lake W of Raleigh and E of Pittsboro. Parking lot turnoff 6.7 miles N of US 64. Marked trail 0.7 miles to observation deck. Owner: U.S. Army Corps of Engineers. Managed by North Carolina Div. of Parks and Recreation and North Carolina Wildlife Resources Commission 919-733-7291.

NORTH DAKOTA

Garrison Dam National Fish Hatchery
Outflow Channel

20-acre site N of Bismarck near hatchery and dam. Winter viewing of bald eagles from beaver pond; fixed blind for viewing and photography. From Riverdale, take ND 200 W over Garrison Dam spillway (about 1 mile) and follow signs toward downstream campgrounds. Park along campground road at S end of hatchery. Walk W cross-country (no marked trail) about 200 yards. Owner: U.S. Army Corps of Engineers, U.S. Fish and Wildlife Service 701-654-7451.

Riverdale Wildlife Management Area

2,197 acres of forest and grassland associated with the Missouri River. More than 15 wintering bald eagles visible from trail or along river from mid-Dec. through Feb. Portable blinds welcome. Foot traffic only; vehicle traffic prohibited. From Riverdale, go W on ND 200 to gravel road just before Garrison Dam spillway (about 0.5 miles); turn S. Road gradually turns W; take second road that turns S for 0.5 miles; turn E or W to management area. From parking lot, follow service road trail S 0.5 miles. Trail turns W toward river for another 0.75 miles. Contact: North Dakota Game and Fish 701-654-7475.

OHIO

Ottawa National Wildlife Refuge

At latest count, 32 bald eagles were staging in the 1,000 acres of habitat in this 6,000-acre complex. Best viewing: Aug. and Sept., from walking trails through marsh and along estuary. Off OH 2, 15 miles E of Toledo. Owner: U.S. Fish and Wildlife Service. Contact: Crane Creek Wildlife Research Station 419-898-0960.

Pickerel Creek State Wildlife Area

2,000 acres SE of Toledo; up to 15 staging eagles. Best viewing: from roads around area and just inside entrance, Aug. and Sept. Off US 6 about 8 miles E of Fremont. Contact: Crane Creek Wildlife Research Station 419-898-0960.

OKLAHOMA

As many as 1,000 eagles spend winters on Oklahoma's lakes and rivers. The Oklahoma Nongame Wildlife Program offers two brochures, *The Bald Eagle in Oklahoma*, and *Oklahoma Bald Eagle Viewing*, which contains a tour schedule updated each winter. Surveys and tours are a cooperative effort of the Nongame Wildlife Program, U.S. Fish & Wildlife Service, National Wildlife Federation, U.S. Army Corps of Engineers, Tulsa Audubon Society, Oklahoma Ornithological Society, and Oklahoma Gas and Electric. Contact: Nongame Wildlife Program, Oklahoma Dept. of Wildlife Conservation, 1801 N. Lincoln, Oklahoma City, OK 73105 405-521-4616.

OREGON

Bald Eagle Conference

Held in Klamath Falls in Feb. during President's Day weekend, the Bald Eagle Conference is sponsored by the Klamath Audubon Society and presented by the National Audubon Society, Oregon Dept. of Fish and Wildlife, U.S. Fish and Wildlife Service, Oregon Eagle Foundation, and Oregon Institute of Technology and Associated Students of OIT. Purpose: To share information, increase awareness, and gain understanding of wildlife resources, especially the bald eagle. Directed at layperson; events, including viewing, Fri. through Sun. Fee; space limited. Contact: Klamath Basin Audubon Society, P.O. Box 354, Klamath Falls, OR 97601.

Bear Valley National Wildlife Refuge/Lower Klamath National Wildlife Refuge

This 4,178-acre valley just N of California is a night roosting area for wintering bald eagles. Watch the "fly out" at dawn when eagles head to Lower Klamath to feed. Approximately 300 eagles Dec. through Feb. Take US 97 S from Worden. Turn W onto road to Keno (after Worden Cafe). Cross railroad tracks and take unmarked gravel road to little valley leading into Bear Valley. Watch fly out from car. Contact: U.S. Fish and Wildlife Service 916-667-2231. (See California section for information on Lower Klamath National Wildlife Refuge. To Lower Klamath from Oregon, go S from Klamath Falls 19 miles on US 97. At state border turn E on CA 161. Headquarters 4 miles S on Hill Rd. off CA 161.)

Crane Prairie Reservoir

6 pairs of bald eagles nest in this 10,600-acre site in the Cascade Mountains. Pairs remain year-round. Best viewing: late Apr. through Sept. from boat; also from docks or lakeshore. Hiking trail leads to reservoir. S 15 miles from Bend on US 97. Turn right at Sunriver turnoff (Forest Rd 40) for 21 miles to Forest Rd 46. Turn S and watch for campgrounds. Trail to reservoir begins 0.5 miles S of Quinn River Campground on Forest Rd. 46. Contact: USDA Forest Service 503-388-5664.

Oak Springs Fish Hatchery

A steep canyon along the Deschutes River SE of The Dalles, along which, Dec. through Feb., 1 to 5 bald eagles fish and roost in the tall trees. Numbers peak in Jan. Best viewing: park car just before railroad tracks, or view from fish hatchery. From Maupin drive 6 miles N on US 197. Turn E 3 miles at fish hatchery sign. Contact: Oregon Dept. of Fish and Wildlife 503-395-2546.

Sauvie Island Wildlife Area

From a few to 30 wintering bald eagles visit this 12,000-acre area from Dec. through Mar. to feed on waterfowl. Best viewing: from Reeder Rd., which parallels refuge. To wildlife area, go W 10 miles from Portland on US 30. Cross Sauvie Island Bridge and travel N 2 miles. Headquarters on right just past the NW Reeder Rd. junction. Entry restricted Oct. through Apr. Oregon Dept. of Fish and Wildlife 503-621-3488.

Twilight Creek Eagle Sanctuary

A single pair of bald eagles nests at Twilight Creek, part of the Columbia River estuary, from about Mar. through Sept. Other bald eagles may also be seen. Viewing platform over intertidal marshes of Cathlamet Bay affords views of foraging eagles. To platform, take old Hwy 30 to Burnside (between Svensen and the John Day River). Respect private property. Contact: CREST (Columbia River Estuary Task Force) 503-325-0435.

Upper Crooked Bald Eagle Viewing Tour

As many as 50 wintering bald eagles congregate in the Upper Crooked River valley NE of Bend Dec. through Apr. Numbers peak in Mar. Best viewing: from the Paulina Hwy, look for eagles in trees along river or soaring overhead. Go E 1 mile from Prineville on US 26. Turn S on the Paulina Hwy 25 miles past Post following the Crooked River. Owner: private, Bureau of Land Management 503-447-4115.

PENNSYLVANIA

Middle Creek Wildlife Management Area

5,000 acres N of Lancaster, with nonbreeding bald eagles Mar. to Sept. By mid-summer, 2 to 3 eagles may be viewed from visitor center or from auto tour pullouts around lake. Look for birds on snags in lake. From PA Turnpike, take exit 21 onto PA 272 N 3 miles to traffic light. Left on PA 897 N about 14 miles to Kleinfeltersville. After stop sign, left onto Hopeland Rd. for 2 miles to visitor center. Contact: Pennsylvania Game Commission 717-733-1512.

Pymatuning Reservoir

5 pairs of bald eagles begin nesting on the state's largest lake in Feb., and most remain year-round. Peak viewing of nests in Apr. Spotting scopes sometimes set up at visitor center; indoor educational programs and tours available. Take I-79 S from Erie to Meadville exit. Go to Conneaut Lake and on to Linesville. At light, turn left and go 0.5 miles past hatchery to entrance. Contact: Pennsylvania Game Commission 814-683-5545.

RHODE ISLAND

Bald eagles are seen year-round in Rhode Island, with frequent sightings of nonbreeding summer birds. Eagles tend to show up in certain spots, but without consistency in numbers or timing. Contact: Rhode Island Dept. of Environmental Management, Great Swamp Field Headquarters 401-789-0281.

SOUTH CAROLINA

ACE Basin

The Ashepoo, Combahee, and Edisto rivers meet on the Atlantic coast in what is known as the ACE Basin. During winter months, 27 pairs of bald eagles nest in the area, with peak viewing Feb. through Apr. The Nature Conservancy recognizes the ACE Basin as a designated bioreserve project and has been involved with state and federal governments for preservation agreements and land transfers. The Nature Conservancy also has several conservation easement agreements with private land owners in the area. 11,000-acre Bear Island Wildlife Management Area and 8,500-acre Donnelly Wildlife Management Area (South Carolina Wildlife & Marine Resources Dept. 803-844-8957) and ACE Basin National Wildlife Refuge (U.S. Fish and Wildlife Service 803-889-3084) are open to the public.

Santee Cooper Lakes

An area that includes the Cooper River and lakes Marion and Moultrie, SE of Columbia. 17 pairs of bald eagles nest around the lakes. Best viewing: Feb. and Mar. from shoreline, Santee Dam, and hiking trails in designated areas. Owner: Santee Cooper-South Carolina Public Service Authority. State and federal agencies manage the area as undeveloped habitat under land-lease agreements. Trail access to lakes from 2,828-acre Santee Cooper Wildlife Management Area (South Carolina Wildlife & Marine Resources 803-825-3387) and from 15,000-acre Santee National Wildlife Refuge (U.S. Fish and Wildlife 803-478-2217). Contact for general information: Santee Cooper-Land Div. 803-761-4068.

SOUTH DAKOTA

Karl E. Mundt National Wildlife Refuge/Fort Randall Dam

From Oct. through Feb., bald eagles winter at the refuge and dam along the Missouri River in SE South Dakota near Nebraska. Refuge closed to public, but an interpretive sign is located downriver from powerhouse below dam, where just over 140 eagles congregate in a 3-mile stretch to feed on fish and waterfowl. Numbers peak in Jan. and Feb. From Pickstown, travel W on US 46, cross Fort Randall Dam, and go to powerhouse below dam. Just before security gate, turn right on blacktop road heading downriver (S) about 0.25 miles. Road deadends at interpretive sign. Contact: U.S. Army Corps of Engineers 605-487-7845; U.S. Fish and Wildlife Service 605-487-7603.

Oahe Dam

20 to 25 bald eagles frequent two areas below Oahe Dam on the Missouri River from early Nov. through mid-Mar. Peak times depend on weather. By car, go through Downstream North (800 acres) campgrounds to view eagles along river. Downstream South (60 acres) is closed to all but foot traffic; park at closed gate and walk down road to water to see eagles feeding or perched in trees across river. Eagle Awareness Day yearly in early Jan.; educational and guided viewing opportunities. Oahe Dam is 6 miles N of Pierre on SD 1804 or SD 1806. Contact: U.S. Army Corps of Engineers 605-224-5862.

TENNESSEE

Dale Hollow Lake

A 27,000-acre lake and 24,000 acres of land with winter viewing of up to 70 eagles Oct. through Mar. Best viewing: from 7.3-mile trail between Willow Grove and Lillydale Recreation areas on S side of lake. U.S. Army Corps of

Engineers offers viewing tours in Jan. On I-40 E from Nashville, take exit 280. Travel N on TN 56 through Gainesboro. Turn N on TN 53 through Celina; follow signs to resource manager's office. Contact: U.S. Army Corps of Engineers 615-243-3136.

Land Between the Lakes

This peninsula straddling the Tennessee and Cumberland river valleys in W Tennessee near the state line has over 300 miles of undeveloped shoreline and hosts about 150 bald eagles in winter and 8 nesting pairs in summer. Viewing by boat or car. Peak concentration Dec. to Jan. Annual Eagle Weekends in Feb. From I-24, go W on US 79 37 miles through Clarksville, across Cumberland River Bridge, and through Dover to S entrance. Turn right (N) on TN 100 (The Trace) about 3 miles to S welcome station. Golden Pond Visitor Center and Planetarium about 20 miles further N. Contact: Tennessee Valley Authority 502-924-5602.

Reelfoot Lake

33,000 acres around Reelfoot Lake, near the Missouri border. 150 to 200 bald eagles concentrate along the shore in winter, peaking Dec. to Feb. Reelfoot Lake State Park has viewing tours, pontoon boat tours (spring through fall), and driving and hiking areas. From Tiptonville, drive 2.6 miles E on TN 21/22 to visitor center on left. U.S. Fish & Wildlife/Reelfoot National Wildlife Refuge; Tennessee Wildlife Resources Agency/Reelfoot Wildlife Management Area; Tennessee Dept. of Environment & Conservation, Bureau of Parks and Recreation/Reelfoot Lake State Park 901-253-7756.

TEXAS

Fairfield Lake State Park

An average of 20 bald eagles winters in this 1,400-acre park SE of Dallas. Best viewing: from boat on lake. Viewing

from shore also possible with binoculars or spotting scope. From I-45 take US 84 E to Fairfield. Drive 6 miles NE on FM 488 and FM 2570 to park road 64. Contact: Texas Parks and Wildlife Dept. 903-359-3926.

Lake Buchanan

Bald eagles and many other species of migrating birds winter at 23,500-acre Lake Buchanan NW of Austin. Best viewing: from boat. Several public boat ramps on lake; also, privately owned Vanishing Texas River Cruise offers tours for fee. Reservation recommended 512-756-6986. To dock for cruises, go 3 miles W of Burnet on TX 29 and N on FM 2341 13.5 miles to entrance. Contact: Lower Colorado River Authority 512-473-4083.

Lake Fork Reservoir

This 27,700-acre reservoir attracts about 80 bald eagles from Nov. to Mar. Viewing from shore or boat. Take US 80 E from Dallas to Mineola. Take TX 37 N to Quitman and TX 154 W to dam. Contact: Sabine River Authority 903-878-2262.

Lake of the Pines

More than 30 bald eagles winter at this 18,700-acre lake in the state's NE corner near Louisiana. Best viewing: from dam overlook; also from boat or shore. From TX 49 NW from Jefferson take US 59 W about 3 miles. Go W on FM 729 to FM 726. Turn S on 726 to dam and south shore parks, or stay on 729 W to north shore parks. Owner: U.S. Army Corps of Engineers. Contact: Lake of the Pines Chamber of Commerce 903-755-2597.

UTAH

Farmington Bay Waterfowl Management Area

About 30 to 35 bald eagles (numbers vary greatly) winter Nov. through Mar. at this 10,625-acre site in N Utah.

Auto and walking routes; tours and educational talks. Take W. Bountiful exit off I-15 and follow signs to area. Contact: Utah Div. of Wildlife Resources 801-451-3395 or 801-479-5143.

Ogden Bay Waterfowl Management Area

A 20,000-acre site in N Utah with 30 to 35 bald eagles Nov. through Mar. (numbers vary greatly). Auto and walking tours. Take exit 341 (Roy) off I-15 and get on UT 97 W until it ends. Go N on UT 108 for 0.1 miles and W on UT 98 to Hooper. Continue W on 5500 S, then N on 7500 W. Contact: Utah Div. of Wildlife Resources 801-773-1398 or 801-479-5143.

Ouray National Wildlife Refuge

The Green River flows through 12 miles of this refuge in Utah's NE corner. Typically, up to 80 bald eagles come mid-Nov. through early Jan., then return late Feb. through Mar. They remain all winter if it is mild and the water does not freeze over. Best viewing: from 9.5-mile auto tour route. Go 14 miles W from Vernal on US 40 and turn S on UT 88 for 16 miles to headquarters. Contact: U.S. Fish and Wildlife Service 801-789-0351.

Pariette Waterfowl Refuge

A high of 60 wintering eagles has been counted at this 9,033-acre marsh complex in NW Utah. Best viewing: late Oct. through Nov. and late Feb. through early Mar., from gravel and dirt roads throughout area. Stay off gated roads. Take US 40 to Fort Duchesne and turn S about 5 miles (just past Duchesne River). At the Myton "Y" turn S off road to Myton onto dirt road for 16 miles across Leland Bench to Pariette Wash. Follow signs to overlook. Inquire first about road conditions. Contact: Bureau of Land Management 801-789-1362.

Rush Lake

This 2,000-acre area with its ephemeral lake hosts 30 or more wintering bald eagles Nov. through Mar. Eagles perch in dead trees along road and roost on E side of lake along UT 36. Excellent viewing from highway, which is elevated. Do not stop on road; use pullouts. Bald eagle activities in winter. From Tooele take UT 36 S to Stockton. Continue on UT 36. Contact: Bureau of Land Management 801-977-4300.

Salt Creek Waterfowl Management Area

A 7,050-acre site in N Utah. About 30 to 35 bald eagles can be seen here Nov. through Mar., though number varies. Auto and walking routes. Good viewing of entire area from Compton's Knoll with spotting scope or binoculars. From Corrine go W 8 miles on UT 83. Turn N on gravel surface for 3.5 miles to entrance. Continue 1.2 miles to Compton's Knoll. Contact: Utah Div. of Wildlife Resources 801-854-3610 or 801-479-5143.

Willard Bay-Harold Crane Waterfowl Management Area

About 30 to 35 bald eagles winter at this 12,500-acre site in N Utah from Nov. through Mar. (number varies). Good viewing from walking routes. From I-15 take exit 354 (Willard Bay, Pleasant View). Turn W on 4000 N and drive to S marina of Willard Bay; walk-in access only. For vehicle access, drive to end of 4000 N, to gravel road. Additional access: from I-15 take exit 347 to UT 39 W. Turn N on 6700 W to walk-in access. Contact: Utah Div. of Wildlife Resources 801-479-5143.

VERMONT

Harriman Station

About 5 eagles spend Dec. through Apr. by this powerhouse below a dam on the Deerfield River W of Brattleboro.

On I-91, take exit 3. Go W 20 miles until road crosses Deerfield River in Readsboro. Travel S on River Rd 1 mile. Contact: New England Power Co. 603-448-2200.

North Monroe Bridge

About 11 bald eagles summer on the island S of this bridge from Jul. through Aug. The bridge spans the Connecticut River at the N end of McIndoes Reservoir, S of St. Johnsbury. Take exit 18 off I-91. Go S on US 5 0.25 miles. North Monroe Bridge on left. Pullout before bridge; park and walk across bridge to view. Viewing also good from adjacent roads, NH 135, and roads between E. Barnet and Lower Waterford. Contact: New England Power Co. 603-448-2200.

Vernon, Bellows Falls, and Wilder Dams

These hydroelectric dams, all within 75 miles of each other, keep water on the Connecticut River open during even the coldest months allowing bald eagles to fish. One or two eagles below each dam any time from Dec. through Apr. Vernon Dam (S of Brattleboro): take I-91 to US 5 and go N; turn S on VT 142 7 miles to dam. Bellows Falls Dam: in downtown Bellows Falls off US 5. Wilder Dam (near White River Junction): take exit 12 off I-91. Follow US 5 N 1.9 miles. Turn right on Depot St., left on Norwich St., and right on Passumpsic Ave. Contact: New England Power Co. 603-448-2200.

VIRGINIA

Caledon Natural Area

From mid-June through early Sept., bald eagles roost, forage, and perch in these 2,579 acres on the Potomac River and marsh E of Fredericksburg. Highest concentration of summering eagles in area: 35 to 40 off shoreline, up to 65 including buffer area. Ranger-led tours mid-June through Labor Day, Thurs. to Sun., 10am and 2pm; fee. Arrange group tours in advance. From US 301 in King George County, take VA 206 W 4 miles to VA 218 W. About 1 mile to park. Contact: Virginia Dept. of Conservation and Recreation 703-663-3861.

Mason Neck National Wildlife Refuge/Mason Neck State Park

8,000-acre peninsula on the Potomac River S of Alexandria has winter viewing of 50 to 60 bald eagles (less than 20 in summer). Best viewing: in refuge, from Great Marsh Trail; in park, from Bay View and Kane's Creek trails. At junction with US 1, go E on VA 242 (Gunston Rd.) to wildlife refuge. Follow High Point Rd., to right, to state park. Owner (refuge): U.S. Fish and Wildlife Service 703-690-1297. Owner (park): Virginia Dept. of Conservation and Recreation 703-550-0960.

WASHINGTON

Methow Wildlife Area

16,000 acres of shrub-steppe and forest habitats W of Colville Indian Reservation. Bald eagle viewing along Methow River; winter viewing between Winthrop and Twisp. Take WA 153 to WA 20. Turn NW to Twisp and on to Winthrop. Contact: Washington Dept. of Wildlife 509-754-4624.

North Fork Nooksack River

Bald eagles concentrate along the Nooksack River (E of Bellingham) from Kendall to Deming (10 miles) Oct. to Mar.; peaks of over 100 Dec./early Jan. Best viewing: from Nooksack Salmon Hatchery and Welcome Bridge on Mosquito Lake Rd. From Kendall go 1 mile S on North Fork Rd. to hatchery; bridge 5 miles farther S. DO NOT PARK IN FRONT OF WELCOME FIRE STATION. Owner: Washington Dept. of Fisheries 206-428-1520, and private land.

San Juan Island: Cattle Point

Much of this island W of Anacortes is a national historic park. Bald eagles present year-round. Best viewing: from Cattle Point, about 10 acres in the far SE. Look for birds roosting in tall trees or soaring near channel between San Juan and Lopez islands. From Friday Harbor, take San Juan Valley Rd. SW. Left (S) on Douglas Rd. Left (W) on Little Rd. Take Cattle Point Rd. S to Cattle Point. Parking area. Owner: Washington Dept. of Natural Resources. Contact: National Park Service, San Juan Island National Historic Park 206-378-2240 or bald eagle biologist 206-775-1311.

Skagit River Bald Eagle Natural Area

Bald eagle viewing Nov. through mid-Mar. on 8 miles of the Skagit River between Rockport and Marblemount. Largest concentration (over 450 in mid-Jan) corresponds with chum salmon spawn. Best viewing: from Washington Eddy lookout 1 mile E of Rockport on WA 20, and a highway pullout 1.3 miles further. Also from Skagit View Trail at Rockport State Park. Visitor regulations. The Nature Conservancy steward is available for presentations and discussion. Upper Skagit Bald Eagle Festival information 206-853-7009. From Seattle, take I-5 N to exit 230. Follow WA 20 36 miles through Burlington to Rockport. Owners: The Nature Conservancy, Washington Field Office 206-343-4344; Washington Dept. of Wildlife.

WEST VIRGINIA

Potomac Eagle Train

A private company offers a 3-hour narrated train ride along the South Branch of the Potomac River, in the NE arm of the state, on the South Branch Valley Railroad. Train passes through narrow valley known as "the Trough." Bald eagles present year-round. Nests clearly visible in May and June from train's open-air gondola. Rides year-round from Wappocomo Station, 1 mile N of Romney. Contact: The Potomac Eagle 304-822-7464.

WISCONSIN

Nelson Dewey State Park

For 100 miles along the Mississippi River from La Crosse to Dubuque, Iowa, there may be 650 wintering bald eagles. Nelson Dewey State Park and Cassville are on a 2-mile stretch of the river, where a Wisconsin Power and Light plant keeps water open in winter. Eagles present mid-Dec. to mid-Mar.; peak late Jan./early Feb. In Cassville, view from platforms above river in park and from boat landing at S end of Riverside Park near old Dairyland Power Plant. Cassville's Bald Eagle Days last weekend in Jan. To park, take WI 133 N from Cassville. At edge of town turn left on County VV; entrance 1 mile on right. Contact: Wisconsin Dept. of Natural Resources 608-725-5374.

Petenwell Dam

Wintering bald eagles can be seen on open water at least a mile below this dam E of La Crosse near I-90. Three observation areas. Stop at parking areas E and W of bridge over Wisconsin River on WI 21. Eagles visible upstream. Drive W from bridge; take 19th St W about 0.2 miles, and 18th Ave N for 0.75 miles. Look just below dam on W side of river for eagles. Also, observation platform near power plant. Contact: Wisconsin River Power Co. 608-565-7961.

Sauk Prairie Eagle Viewing Site

As many as 200 bald eagles winter in this area about 25 miles NW of Madison from mid-Dec. to mid-Feb. because dam on Lower Wisconsin River keeps water open. Observation platform with spotting scope; if not viewing from platform, please remain in car. Some weekends in peak season, volunteers provide interpretive information at platform. Near Sauk City, take US 12 N across Wisconsin River. Turn right immediately on Water St. for 1.4 miles to public parking lot near Fire House Restaurant in Prairie du Sac. Owner: Village of Prairie du Sac. Managed by Ferry Bluff Eagle Council and Wisconsin Dept. of Natural Resources. Contact: Prairie du Sac Chamber of Commerce 608-643-4168.

WYOMING

Bighorn River

From Dec. through early Mar., about 25 to 50 bald eagles winter along a stretch of the Bighorn River from Greybull to Thermopolis, NW of Casper. Follow WY 433 along the river. US 20 connects Greybull and Thermopolis.

Buffalo Bill State Park

About 11,000 acres just SW of Cody. In Mar. and Apr. and in Oct. and Nov., migrating eagles frequent the inlets of Buffalo Bill Reservoir. Some eagles also winter Nov. through Mar. Good viewing of perching birds from either end of reservoir on North and South forks of Shoshone River. Drive the North Fork Hwy (US 14/16/20), or WY 1501 along the South Fork. Good viewing from gravel roads off these roads. The state of Wyoming has a management agreement with the Bureau of Reclamation 307-587-9227.

Jackson Canyon

See a concentration of wintering bald eagles along the North Platte River from the Jackson Canyon pullout, off I-25 SW of Casper. A roost of about 50 eagles from mid-Nov. through mid-Mar. (numbers vary throughout summer). View from parking lot so as not to disturb birds. Actual roost on private land.

Snake River

A stretch of the Snake River just N and S of Jackson, from Jackson Lake to the Idaho border. Bald eagles year-round; about 30 pairs in summer and 50 to 100 birds in winter. In summer, float down river through Grand Teton National Park to see eagles. Drive along US 191 N and S of Jackson, or on road along river in Grand Teton National Park. Pullouts along the way. Contact: Grand Teton National Park Headquarters 307-739-3300.

Woodruff Narrows Reservoir

In winter, over 200 bald eagles may congregate at the lower/north end of this reservoir below the dam on the Bear River, in the SW corner of the state near Utah. Follow WY 89 NW about 13 miles from Evanston to the Utah border. Enter Utah briefly and follow County 101 0.5 miles back into Wyoming. Follow the road to the left for just under 7 miles. Again, follow the road to the left 2 miles along a north-running fence. Some of this land privately owned.

Yellowstone National Park

From Dec. through Feb., about 8 to 10 bald eagles winter on the Madison River in Yellowstone National Park. To the river from within the park, take the West Yellowstone entrance road to Madison Junction. About 20 summering eagles may be seen near Hayden Valley and around Yellowstone Lake. Nesting eagles present from May through Oct. Enter park from E at Cody. View from points around Yellowstone Lake or continue N on Grand Loop Rd. in Hayden Valley. Contact: Yellowstone National Park 307-344-7381.

ABOUT THE PHOTOGRAPHER/ AUTHOR

Frank Oberle, the premier photographer for this book, may be the most prolific bald eagle photographer in the country. *Audubon, Sports Illustrated, National Geographic, Nature Conservancy,* and *National Wildlife* are just a few of the publications in which his eagle images have appeared. Shooting photos like Oberle's takes as much patience as it does skill. Oberle's images capture perfectly the grace, artistry, and beauty of bald eagles.

Greg Breining has traveled around the world, from desolate Siberia to tropical Jamaica, in search of stories for books and magazines. He writes on subjects as diverse as bison, fossils, and canoes for *Sports Illustrated, Nature Conservancy, Audubon, Sierra,* and other magazines. *Return of the Eagle* is his seventh book.

126

ACKNOWLEDGMENTS

The publisher would like to thank the following organizations and individuals for their help in gathering site information for the Bald Eagle Viewing Directory.

Arkansas Game & Fish-John B. Welch

Connecticut Department of Environmental Protection, Wildlife Division

Klamath Basin Bald Eagle Conference, c/o Oregon Department of Fish and Wildlife-Ralph Opp

Massachusetts Division of Fisheries and Wildlife-Bill Davis

Minnesota Department of Natural Resources, Nongame Wildlife Program

Missouri Department of Natural Resources

Montana Fish, Wildlife & Parks-Dennis Flath

Nevada Division of Wildlife-Gary Herron

New Jersey Division of Fish, Game and Wildlife, Endangered and Nongame Species Program

New York State Department of Environmental Conservation, Endangered Species Unit-Peter Nye

Oklahoma Nongame Wildlife Program

The Nature Conservancy

State of Utah, Wildlife Resources-Robert Walters

West Virginia Division of Natural Resources

Wisconsin Department of Natural Resources

Bob Berry, Cindy Gilgore Brown, Ellen Campbell, John Carr, Susan Cerulean, Jeanne L. Clark, Jim Cole, Mark Duda, Hank Fischer, Gary L. Graham, Bob Hernborde, Mike Jacobson, Dan Jensen, Mary Judd, Joe LaTourrette, Don MacCarter, Terry McEneaney, Laura Mitchell, John Ragonese, Charles Roe, Raymond Rustem, Phil T. Seng (DJ Case & Associates), Gary Simmons, June Vaughn (Conowingo Recreation Project), Lynn Wallen, R.T. Wallen, Bob Walters, and James A. Yuskavitch.